CW00537571

MOTHERING AS A METAPHOR FOR MINISTRY

This is a wise, kind, intelligent book which many (men as well as women) will find illuminates their experience of ministry and helps them cope with overload, anxiety and the perennial guilt trap which is often their lot.

Angela Tilby, Christ Church Cathedral, Oxford

This imaginative, thoughtful and thought-provoking book is a gift to all those who are seeking new language to express what ministry might mean in the twenty-first century. The exploration of motherhood as a metaphor for ministry opens up not only new language but a whole new way of ministering.

Paula Gooder, Freelance Writer, Canon Theologian, and Lecturer in Biblical Studies

Drawing together original research which weaves together ideas from theology, philosophy, feminism and writing on mothering and child development, Emma Percy affirms and encourages aspects of good practice in ministry that are in danger of being overlooked because they are neither well-articulated nor valued. Offering a fresh look at parish ministry, this book uses a maternal metaphor to provide an integrated image of being and doing.

The metaphor of mothering is used to explore the relational aspect of parish ministry which needs to value particularity and concrete contingent responsiveness. Percy suggests virtues that need to be cultivated to guard against the temptations to intrusive or domineering styles of care on the one hand or passive abnegation of responsibility on the other. Parish ministry cannot be understood in terms of tangible productivity; different ways of understanding success and evaluating priorities need to be developed. The book suggests ways of being 'good enough' clergy who can find the right balance between caring for people and communities whilst encouraging and acknowledging the maturity of others.

Ashgate Contemporary Ecclesiology

Series Editors
Martyn Percy, Ripon College Cuddesdon, Oxford, UK
D. Thomas Hughson, Marquette University, USA
Bruce Kaye, Charles Sturt University, Australia

Series Advisory Board
James Nieman; Sathi Clarke; Gemma Simmonds CJ; Gerald West;
Philip Vickeri; Helen Cameron; Tina Beattie; Nigel Wright; Simon Coleman

The field of ecclesiology has grown remarkably in the last decade, and most especially in relation to the study of the contemporary church. Recently, theological attention has turned once more to the nature of the church, its practices and proclivities, and to interpretative readings and understandings on its role, function and ethos in contemporary society.

This new series draws from a range of disciplines and established scholars to further the study of contemporary ecclesiology and publish an important cluster of landmark titles in this field. The Series Editors represent a range of Christian traditions and disciplines, and this reflects the breadth and depth of books developing in the Series. This Ashgate series presents a clear focus on the contemporary situation of churches worldwide, offering an invaluable resource for students, researchers, ministers and other interested readers around the world working or interested in the diverse areas of contemporary ecclesiology and the important changing shape of the church worldwide.

Mothering as a Metaphor for Ministry

EMMA PERCY
Trinity College Oxford, UK

ASHGATE

Published by
Ashgate Publishing Limited
Wey Court East
Union Road
Farnham
Surrey, GU9 7PT
England

Ashgate Publishing Company
110 Cherry Street
Suite 3-1
Burlington, VT 05401-3818
USA

www.ashgate.com

British Library Cataloguing in Publication Data
A catalogue record for this book is available from the British Library

The Library of Congress has cataloged the printed edition as follows:
Percy, Emma.
  Mothering as a metaphor for ministry / by Emma Percy.
    pages cm. -- (Ashgate contemporary ecclesiology)
  ISBN 978-1-4094-6691-8 (hardcover : alk. paper) — ISBN 978-1-4094-6692-5 (ebook)
— ISBN 978-1-4094-6693-2 (epub) 1. Pastoral theology—Church of England. 2. Pastoral
theology—Anglican Communion. 3. Church work—Church of England. 4. Church
work—Anglican Communion. 5. Motherhood—Religious aspects—Church of England.
6. Motherhood—Religious aspects—Anglican Communion. I. Title.
  BV4011.3.P465 2013
  253—dc23

2013011285

ISBN 9781409466918 (hbk)
ISBN 9781409466925 (ebk – PDF)
ISBN 9781409466932 (ebk – ePUB)

Printed in the United Kingdom by Henry Ling Limited,
at the Dorset Press, Dorchester, DT1 1HD

For Martyn, Ben and Joe

Contents

Acknowledgements

My initial writing about motherhood and ministry came out of a sabbatical spent in Hartford Seminary, CT, USA. My thanks to the then Dean the Very Reverend Professor Ian Markham for his hospitality and encouragement. Dr Karen Kilby from the Department of Theology at Nottingham University agreed to supervise further research and her incredible support and thorough scrutiny enabled me to enjoy the process of completing the PhD which forms the basis of this book. My thanks also to the Women's Ministry Fund which generously supported my tuition fees.

Canon Anthony Hulbert, my training Incumbent, modelled a truly virtuous parish ministry. I thank him and the parish of St Andrew's Bedford, who supported me through the beginnings of my ministerial and maternal practices.

Many friends have helped in shaping the ideas in this book, in particular Reverend Anne Stevens, Canon Maggie McLean, Kate Quarry and Reverend Dr Karin Voth Harman. My colleagues at Trinity College have been generous in their interest.

The people of Holy Trinity, Millhouses, Sheffield where I was parish priest for seven years shaped much of my thinking. It was a privilege to work together to be the church in that place.

Ben and Joe are the wonderful young men whose mother I am. Seeing them develop towards adulthood is truly inspiring.

Finally and most importantly I thank Martyn for all the conversations, joys, struggles and love we have shared in building a home, living in the vicarage, doing theology and endeavouring to live out our vocations. I am greatly blessed.

Emma Percy
February 2013

Introduction

Many parish clergy have to contend with the assumption that they only really work on Sundays when the reality is that they are working extremely long hours and can often feel overwhelmed by all that there is to do. However, actually explaining what it is that they do is not easy. The role of a parish priest does not easily correlate to modern patterns of work. Increasingly, as a wider culture of aims and objectives, realisable targets and action plans impinges on the church, parish priests can be left feeling a mixture of frustration, confusion and even guilt about how to justify their ministry. In the past it seems that no one needed to justify or articulate what it was that clergy did but in today's world and today's church we need to find a language to talk about what a vicar does. The majority of recent books written for clergy acknowledge the difficulty in articulating what clergy do. Historical changes in the role of the parish priest as a profession and theological debates about ordination prompted by ecumenical discussions raise questions about the significance of the ordained. The increase in authorised lay ministries and non-traditional patterns of ordained ministry raise questions about collaboration. All of this can leave clergy wondering what it is to be a priest. Increasingly the language of leadership is used rather than of priesthood and managerial models are offered which feel inadequate and inappropriate in the experience of many priests.

It is my contention that we need to use more imaginative language and to find metaphors for ministry that can provide clergy with models of working that relate better to their day-to-day experience. To use a metaphor is not to say that one thing is another but that it is like another in a way that can open up and enrich our understanding. This book explores one such metaphor; parish ministry is like mothering. Through looking in more depth at the role of mothering, which is both a relationship and an activity, and then using this as a metaphor for parish ministry, I suggest we can enrich our understanding of the latter and find a language to cherish many aspects of good practice that appear to be side-lined under the prevalent leadership models.

Mothering and parish ministry are both aspects of human activity that Christians would affirm as valuable but both are surprisingly under-articulated. As I will explore in the book this is partly because mothering has been understood as a natural outworking of a female instinct and ministry an outworking of grace. These assumptions have tended to undermine the learning necessary in both practices. This book will challenge some of these assumptions, seeking to offer a more nuanced theology of ministry and mothering, one in which the practitioner in each case needs to develop ways of thinking and acting, shaped by certain virtues, in order to be good enough. It is not an empirical study of either mothers or priests. Nor is it a study of how mothers function as parish priests. It does, however, draw on my own experiences of being a mother and a parish priest – experiences out of which the original thinking and exploration began. As our language is gendered I have chosen to refer to a priest as female and a child as male in the text. However, in doing so I am assuming that the priest or child could be male or female it is simply easier to use one pronoun. This book aims to offer insights for men and women engaged in parish ministry, those who have and do not have children, providing a metaphor to open up their thinking and suggest a richer language for them to reflect on their own experience.

As I said above, mothering is both a relationship and an activity. It brings together being and doing in a complex, intertwined way of working. Mothers are mothers by dint of their relationship to specific children so that mothering is grounded in particularity; I am Ben and Joe's mother. My mothering relationship is then lived out in what I do as a mother for and with them. I am actively involved in mothering them, though not all the time. And in this loving, nurturing and caring I collaborate with other people who are not their mother but who share in different ways in the practice of mothering them. Plenty of the necessary tasks can be shared and undertaken by a number of different people, but the children also require the knowledge that my relatedness is trustworthy, that I am there for them and I will ensure that the necessary care will be provided. Ministry too is a complex mixture of being and doing, a relationship and an activity. We minister to particular people and communities not to generic ones. There are expectations about the kinds of activities required of a priest in order to sustain and enhance the relationship into which they are called. She must be this people's priest and she must ensure that in collaboration with others they are ministered to responsively and appropriately.

This book offers an extended reflection on this kind of relational activity and posits an analogous relationship between the contingent nature of the practice of mothering on the one hand, and ministry on the other. This contingency arises out of the reality that the work of mothers and priests is fundamentally connected to specific people who are constantly adapting and changing. Sara Ruddick's *Maternal Thinking*[1] uses philosophical ideas of practice and virtue to better articulate mothering. Her insights have shaped my thinking and will provide a way of using a maternal metaphor to articulate the demands, virtues and temptations of the practice of ministry. My intention is to illuminate good practice in ministry and to suggest attitudes, virtues and cognitive capacities that can aid good practice.

Part I will look at the language of ordained ministry. The first two chapters will outline some of the theological difficulties we have in talking about ordination with a particular focus on issues in the Church of England. There is a tendency to express ordination in either ontological or functional terms, both of which make it difficult to understand the relational aspects of ministry. I suggest that if ministry is understood ecclesiologically, as belonging to the church, it becomes easier to focus on the relational role of clergy to the particular parish they are called to.

---

[1]   Sara Ruddick, *Maternal Thinking* (Boston 1989).

Parish priests are to be 'in charge' but this should be understood as taking on the responsibility to care; they have the charge, or cure, of souls. What is needed is a relational metaphor that reflects this caring relationship. In Chapter 3 I will show how the relational metaphor of mothering has been used in both scripture and historical writings to enhance an understanding of Christian ministry. In chronicling such usage it becomes clear that, although mothering is a female term, it has been used by men to think metaphorically about their ministry.

Part II will look at questions of gender, and the theory and practice of mothering. I will challenge the idea that mothering is an essentially feminine instinctual response and suggest that this understanding of mothering has been a factor in dismissing the thinking behind the activity. Instead I will explore mothering as a learned practice arising out of a relationship which carries with it the responsibility to care. This caring relationship is developed through attachment and appropriate responsiveness and is an inter-subjective relationship. Such a relationship allows for two subjects even when it is asymmetric; one being more dependent on the other. Ruddick's exploration of maternal practice with three competing demands offers a language of virtues and appropriate cognitive capacities. Alongside her thinking I also use the philosophy of Hannah Arendt and her categories of labouring work and action outlined in *The Human Condition.*[2] Mothering is primarily an activity of 'labouring' and 'action' with less of the 'work' which is characterised by blueprints, tangible ends and measurable outcomes. Mothering is a meaningful learnt practice which intricately intertwines the labouring practicalities of caring for a child and the complex action involved in helping a unique individual grow up towards maturity.

Part III will take the insights from mothering and talk about how ministry is in many ways a like practice. The demands of ministry present similar challenges albeit in a very different relationship. Clergy have a responsibility to help individuals and communities grow up into the full stature of Christ. In doing so they engage in labouring activity which is often shared, maintaining the Christian lives of those they have in their charge. This labouring is complexly interwoven with the action of creating webs of relationships between people and between individuals, communities and God.

I note Naomi Stadlen's book on mothering, *What Mothers Do: Especially When it Looks like Nothing*,[3] and her assertion that mothers can find it difficult to properly assess the worth of what they do, let alone have it recognised externally, because they do not have the language to talk about it. This difficulty in articulating much of what is being done is also true of those engaged in parish ministry. Therefore I identify a number of ways of being and acting that are central to good practice in ministry and through imagery and language drawn from mothering seek to better articulate learned skills. This can then begin to counteract the tendency of many

---

[2]   Hannah Arendt, *The Human Condition* (Chicago 1958; 2nd edn 1998).

[3]   Naomi Stadlen, *What Mothers Do: Especially When it Looks like Nothing* (London 2004).

clergy to under value the good they are doing. Such undervaluing can mean that they do not find the necessary pleasure and affirmation in their work to sustain them through the ambiguities and stresses of a job that, on many levels, can never be completed. In seeking to use a maternal imagery to articulate the intertwined relationship and activity of ministry, I aim to provide a more coherent way of developing and assessing good practice. Clergy need to be good enough in their role as a parish priest, good enough to enable the people in their care to mature in faith and understanding.

PART I
Exploring Ministry

Chapter 1
Ministry: Ontology and Function

Since ordained ministry is central to the Church of England's ecclesiology it might be assumed that there is consensus over what constitutes ministry and how the ordained and the non-ordained collaborate constructively. Instead we find that these questions are underdeveloped. In this chapter I will outline how different understandings of the origin of the ordained ministry have implications for how collaborative ministry is understood. If the origin of the priesthood is located in a 'moment of creation'[1] by Christ, for instance the calling of the Apostles or their commissioning, then ordination precedes the emergence of the Church. Theologies that take this as a starting point tend to follow an essentialist view of ordination; the ordained become distinct, set apart and even ontologically changed through the grace of God at ordination. However, this understanding can lead to problems in articulating the relationship between the ordained and the wider Church and particular issues in talking about collaborative patterns of ministry. Alternatively, the role of the ordained can be understood as emerging from the early Church in a more 'evolutionary' way. Thus the clergy have arisen out of the Church's need for leadership and order. In this understanding the ordained should, ideally, serve the needs of the Church and adapt as the Church adapts over time. However, this theology must guard against a purely functional understanding of ministry, which loses sight of the sacramental nature of the role. In exploring these questions it is important to note the kinds of imagery and language used about the ordained. Often the language used is connected to an underlying theology that may no longer be apparent or appropriate.

Apostolic Succession and the Essential Difference of the Ordained

The Anglican theologian Anthony Hanson makes this comment about the Church of England's theology of ministry.

> Anglicans in the past have either leaned heavily on the theory of Apostolic Succession to supply them with a theology of the ministry, or been quite content to have no particular doctrine of the ministry at all.[2]

---

[1]   In using the language of creation and evolution I am drawing on the work of Martyn Percy in *Clergy: The Origin of Species* (London 2006).

[2]   Anthony Hanson, *Church, Sacraments and Ministry* (Oxford 1975), p. 101.

The ordination practice of the Church of England, with its emphasis on Episcopal lineage, highlights the importance of succession. The authority to minister is passed from one generation of the ordained to the next.[3] These rites are shaped by the particular history of the Reformation in England and the continuity between the Roman Catholic Church and the emergent Anglican Church. One way of understanding this continuity is the theology of Apostolic Succession which posits an unbroken line from Christ's setting apart of the Apostles to present-day ordinations. This continuity of orders became central to Anglo-Catholic understandings of ordination, particularly after Pope Leo XIII declared Anglican orders null and void in a Vatican document of 1896.[4] However, the doctrine is about more than simply the transmission of authority. It carries with it a particular understanding of the origin and character of the ordained. Hanson's comment that Anglicans have *leaned* on this theory conveys the reality that it has often been adhered to without a proper understanding of its underlying theology.

The theology of Apostolic Succession, like some more Protestant theologies of ministry, locates the origin of the ordained before the emergence of the Church, in Jesus' calling and commissioning of the Apostles. In the Catholic tradition, Jesus' resurrection encounter with Peter is particularly significant, as he is thrice told to feed or tend Jesus' lambs.[5] It is argued that as Jesus commissioned Peter and the other Apostles so, in turn, they commissioned their successors, through the laying on of hands, down to the bishops and priests of the modern Church. A Catholic theology emphasises the importance of the continuity of ordination; a more Protestant theology would look for conformity to New Testament patterns. Both would tend to favour a Christological model: the ordained successors of the Apostles are to represent Christ and tend his flock as he himself would do. The ordained ministry is thus instigated by Christ himself and Christ is the pattern and model for the ongoing practice. The ordained are to be like the Good Shepherd, tending the flock entrusted to them and the imagery of bishops and priests being shepherds continues to shape the language and metaphors used about ordained ministry.

Notwithstanding that shepherding and pastoral images have been a rich and fruitful language through the Church's history, such language provides a model that is, on one level at least, fundamentally problematic. Shepherds are of a different species from their sheep, and clearly a superior species. This species difference is not accidental and is not simply a matter of language: it is a fundamental aspect of a theology of ministry that locates the origin of the ordained as separate and prior

---

[3]   Hence the very difficult debates about women bishops. If they are not recognised as real bishops they can threaten the continuity of Apostolic Succession, meaning that all clergy would need some kind of 'pedigree' to show that they had a proper Episcopal lineage.

[4]   *Apostolicae Curae* is the title of the papal bull issued in 1896 by Pope Leo XIII, declaring all Anglican ordinations to be 'absolutely null and utterly void'. www. papalencyclicals.net/Leo13/l13curae (10 November 2011).

[5]   John 21:15–17.

to the emergence of the Church. This theology of difference is spelled out clearly in some of the modern thinking about priesthood in the Roman Catholic Church and particularly in debates about the universal priesthood of all and the ministerial priesthood of the ordained. Clearly, the intention is not to argue for the superiority of clergy, but it is to maintain their essential difference.

The documents on the ministry in the Second Vatican Council used the terminology of a common priesthood of all the baptised and a ministerial priesthood. The two were to be understood as intimately connected but essentially different. The quote below is from *Lumen Gentium*, the document on the Church from the Second Vatican Council:

> Though they differ essentially and not only in degree, the common priesthood of the faithful and the ministerial or hierarchical priesthood are nonetheless ordered one to another; each in its own proper way shares in the one priesthood of Christ.[6]

This common language of priesthood inevitably caused some confusion. Jean Galot writes:

> The phrases 'universal priesthood' and 'ministerial priesthood' can give rise to a confusion: the word 'priesthood' can be taken to refer to a reality identical in both priesthoods with only minor differences appended. But if we consider the data available in the gospels, we realise that a profound difference exists between the two realities involved … It is true of course that Christ is the origin of both priesthoods. However, these derive from Christ along two lines essentially different: each of them in its own special way is a participation in the one priesthood of Christ.[7]

Galot argues that those engaged in the ministerial priesthood are also, as disciples, part of the universal priesthood. However, he also emphasises that the ministerial priesthood is something set apart, with its origins prior to the Church. There is an essential difference or, as it is sometimes expressed, an ontological distinction, that comes about through the sacramental rite of ordination.

It is important to note here the language of difference, which will surface again in this book when considering questions of gender. Debates about how difference is understood in men and women, and whether such differences are essential, highlight the difficulties that we have in discussing difference and the tendency to define one as the opposite of the other, and the privileging of one over the

---

[6]   Dogmatic Constitution on the Church *Lumen Gentium*, solemnly promulgated by His Holiness Pope Paul VI on 21 November 1964. www.vatican.va/archive/hist_councils/ii_vatican_council/documents/vat-ii_const_19641121_lumen-gentium_en (10 November 2012).

[7]   Jean Galot, *Theology of the Priesthood* (San Francisco 1985), pp. 118–19.

other. It is perhaps not surprising that the language of masculine and feminine has been used by some writers to explore the distinctions between the 'universal' and 'ministerial' priesthood. The Church, the universal priesthood, is the feminine bride of Christ, receptive to the ministry of the masculine Christ mediated through male clergy.[8] It is also not surprising that traditionally Catholic and Protestant theologies that locate the origin of the ordained in Christ entrusting his mission to the Apostles tend to oppose the idea of women clergy. The issues of gender will be looked at in more detail later, but what we learn from that debate is that a language of distinction, however much it stresses complementarity and equality of worth, tends to privilege one subject over the other. In terms of priesthood and ministry, the privileging is of the ordained; the ministerial priesthood. The laity or universal priesthood is defined as opposite or complementary to the ordained.

Stephen Pickard argues that the tensions within the language of the ministerial priesthood and universal priesthood are inherent when a Christological model underpins the theology of ministry because they map on to the tensions in understanding the two natures of Christ:

> The common priesthood from below and the representative priesthood from above correspond to the double reality of the humanity and divinity of Christ ... It is hard to resist the conclusion that the two-nature problem in Christology has been transferred into the two priesthoods of the Church, the ordained and the baptised. Given the long and contested history of attempts to develop an adequate account of the two-nature doctrine, it is no surprise that a doctrine of ministry indebted to this Christology will produce unsynthesised antinomies.

---

[8]   A good example of this nuptial imagery being central to salvation and the Eucharist is found in *Inter Insigniores* –'Declaration of the sacred congregation for the doctrine of the faith on the question of the admission of women to the ministerial priesthood' (15 October 1976). www.papalencyclicals.net/Paul06/p6interi (10 November 2011).

For the salvation offered by God to men and women, the union with him to which they are called – in short, the Covenant took on, from the Old Testament Prophets onwards, the privileged form of a nuptial mystery: for God the Chosen People is seen as his ardently loved spouse ... Christ is the Bridegroom; the Church is his bride ... That is why we can never ignore the fact that Christ is a man. And therefore, unless one is to disregard the importance of this symbolism for the economy of Revelation, it must be admitted that, in actions which demand the character of ordination and in which Christ himself, the author of the Covenant, the Bridegroom and Head of the Church, is represented, exercising his ministry of salvation – which is in the highest degree the case of the Eucharist – his role (this is the original sense of the word persona) must be taken by a man. This does not stem from any personal superiority of the latter in the order of values, but only from a difference of fact on the level of functions and service.

The fact that the image of the Church is female in this passage does not lead to any sense that it needs to actually be female in the way that the priest must in representing the bridegroom be male. The symbolism of a female priest could imply imagery of a relationship between the female Church and a feminine Christ, and thus undermine the nuptial image.

> The problem of the relations between the body of Christ and its representative
> ministry; between the ministry and ministries, cannot be unravelled on the basis
> of a defective or incoherent two-nature doctrine of Christ.[9]

Pickard argues that this has implications for the Anglican Church's stated desire to develop collaborative patterns of ministry between the ordained and the laity.[10] If the authority of the ordained resides in their separate priesthood, it is difficult to see how that is shared or enhanced by the ministry of the laity.

It also follows that if the priesthood of the ordained is articulated in the language of Christ's divinity, using imagery like that of the shepherd, the priesthood of all believers tends to be articulated as 'other' and in some sense opposite to the ordained. Thus they become the flock, which is led and which responds by participating rather than initiating. In order to develop collaborative ministry, a different pattern of relationship between the ordained and the wider Church is needed; a more integral relationship, a different understanding of clergy origins and an ecclesiological rather than Christological model for ordination.

The Ministry of the Church and the Emergence of Order

To understand the origin of the ordained from a more 'evolutionary' perspective is not to underplay the significance of the Apostles or the sense that the apostolic faith has been handed on from one generation to the next. Instead the aim is to acknowledge how the early Church began to develop appropriate patterns of leadership *pragmatically*, as well as inspirationally, as it grew and spread. The Acts of the Apostles notes the appointment of the first deacons to deal with a particular problem of order.[11] Although the terminology of episcopacy, presbyters and deacons is used in some New Testament epistles the pattern of Church leadership is not clearly delineated. Over the first few centuries the Church developed a threefold order of ministry using these titles, with recognisable rites of ordination, but these orders had *emerged* from the Church. The origins of ministry are therefore to be found in the life of the Church. They emerge with the blessing of the Apostles and early Church leaders out of the experience of the Church. This pragmatic emergent ministry can be understood as being inspired by the Holy Spirit but that does not imply that the ordained are in essence different from the wider Church. They are authorised to exercise particular functions within the Church, within specified

---

[9] Stephen Pickard, *Theological Foundations for Collaborative Ministry* (Farnham 2009), p. 90.

[10] Pickard links the problems in a two-stranded ministry to a Nestorian Christology, ibid., pp. 112–13.

[11] Acts 6:1–6. In this passage the appointment of seven men as deacons is described as a response to a particular tension within the Church community.

roles. This is the understanding of clergy origins taken by the document *Call to Order*, published by the Church of England in 1989:

> The historical development of this order was gradual and complex, and owed much to forms of ministry already available in Jewish and Gentile cultures as well as to the special needs of time and place. Even when, by the second and third centuries, a threefold order of bishop, presbyter and deacon became the generally accepted pattern, it continued to function differently in different places and different ages.[12]

This report understands ordained ministry as a role that emerged out of the needs of the church and it acknowledges the diversity in the way ministry functioned.

The Roman Catholic theologian Edward Schillebeeckx in two works, *Ministry*[13] and *The Church with a Human Face*,[14] traces the evolving understanding of the role of the ordained. He maintains that whilst the terminology of orders has stayed the same, factors such as monasticism, the changing emphasis on the place of the Eucharist, the Reformation and Counter-Reformation have all played their part in the way ministry has been understood and practised. He particularly notes the shift from the presbyter as the recognised leader of the community, who therefore presides at the Eucharist, to the priest's ability to celebrate the Eucharist as his primary function. This shift led to the practice of private masses where the priest is able to celebrate the Eucharist without a congregation.[15] The Protestant nature of the Church of England means that private masses and the idea of 'absolute' ordination[16] are not part of the tradition, so priesthood is understood subtly differently from the Roman Catholic position. An Anglican priest cannot preside at the Eucharist without a congregation, however small, and Anglicans are always ordained to serve a specific community, thus maintaining the sense of relationship. However, because the language and theology of priesthood is often borrowed from Catholicism, the significance of these differences may be understated. Schillebeeckx's concern is the shift to ordination residing in the person of the priest and in their Eucharistic role rather than in relationship to the actual church community. This underpins a theology that sees the ordained priest as distinct and separate from the shared priesthood of the community.

---

[12]   *Call to Order* (London 1989), para 61.

[13]   Edward Schillebeeckx, *Ministry: A Case for Change* (London 1981).

[14]   Edward Schillebeeckx, *The Church with a Human Face* (London 1985).

[15]   Schillebeeckx, *Ministry*, pp. 56–7.

[16]   Canon 6 of the Council of Chalcedon 451 had said: 'No man is to be ordained without a charge, neither presbyter, nor deacon, nor indeed anyone who is in the ecclesiastical order …'. www.piar.hu/councils/ecum04htm (28 February 2012). To disconnect the ordination from some kind of charge or title was to focus the ordination in the priest absolutely rather than in the relationship between priest and community.

For Schillebeeckx the apostolic tradition resides in the continuity of the Church witnessing to the truth of the apostolic faith. Ordained clergy are one of the ways in which the Church is able to function as the unbroken witness to the apostolic truths of the Christian faith but it is an ecclesial rather than individual continuity. The ordained are not essentially separate from the laity; difference is located in role and function. He was well aware that a socio-historical study of priesthood would lead some to suggest that he was neglecting the sacramental nature of priesthood and reducing it to a functional role. He does not see a contradiction between understanding the ordained as 'an ecclesial function' with the idea that they are a 'gift of God':

> The tension between an ontological sacerdotalist view of the ministry on the one hand and a purely functionalist view on the other must therefore be resolved by a theological view of the church's ministry as a charismatic office, the service of leading the community, and therefore as an ecclesial function within the community and accepted by the community. Precisely in this way it is a gift of God.[17]

It therefore follows that to argue that the ordained ministry has emerged from the Church is not to deny the role of God in its institution and ongoing calling but to acknowledge that it is through the Church as the body of Christ that the Spirit has and continues to work.

Ministry as Ecclesial Function

In emphasising the connection between the ordained and the community of the Church the aim is to understand ministry as belonging to the Church with the ordained having 'an ecclesial function' within the whole. This removes the sense of ontological distinction between the ordained and the lay, but does continue to present linguistic problems about how the ministry of each is to be defined in terms of difference:

> The whole church, as the people of God, has a ministry and priesthood. 'You are a chosen race, a royal priesthood, a holy nation, God's own people' (1 Peter, 2:9). We should notice that this ministry and priesthood belong to the people as a whole. It is understood collectively. It is a mistaken individualism and egalitarianism that talks about the 'priesthood of all believers', as if this priesthood of the people could be divided up into equal shares among all the members of the people. We must never separate ministry and church, for the ministry is to be understood in the context of the church.[18]

---

[17] Schillebeeckx, *Ministry*, p. 70.

[18] John Macquarrie, *Theology, Church and Ministry* (London 1986), p. 157.

John Macquarrie comments thus on the corporate nature of ministry and the inappropriateness of talking about it as if it is somehow divisible. If the apostolic ministry is the ministry of the whole Church, then technically it does not make sense to talk about different ministries but, instead, the language should be about different aspects of the one ministry and differing roles within the collective ministry of the Church.

Jurgen Moltmann in *The Church in the Power of the Spirit* argues that for this collective ministry to be carried out, individuals may be given positions of particular responsibility:

> The general commissioning of the whole congregation will go on to concede a special position and responsibility to the people with special charges, because otherwise the charges cannot be fulfilled.[19]

Those commissioned to take on special responsibilities in the Church do so in order that the community may exercise aspects of the collective ministry. Those commissioned also speak to the community of its connection with the wider Church across space and time. In Moltmann's understanding:

> According to the powers and possibilities available, the charges we have named can be full-time or part-time. They can be carried out by men and women, by the married and the unmarried, by the theologically trained and people without any theological training. They can be exercised by individuals and groups.[20]

This is a clear vision of collaborative patterns of ministry in which all kinds of people are engaged in roles that are collectively serving the kingdom. It offers no distinction between the ordained and the lay and therefore has no need to elaborate on their relationship. Yet clearly he is interested in those who speak to the community of the wider Church; this is not simply a Congregationalist view. It is a pragmatic and functional view in which people take on the charges and roles necessary to make the collective work happen.

The Anglican Church both wants to promote and affirm patterns of collaborative ministry that match the vision Moltmann sets out above, but also wants to maintain a tradition that sees the ordained as sacramental and not simply functional. Denominational authorisation is important for a church to be more than congregational but we have authorised lay ministries thus there is a continuing tension about what differentiates the ordained. There is also a tension about how the ordained and the lay collectively minister together. An ecclesiological understanding of the corporate nature of ministry is constantly undercut by the language of 'two ministries'; the lay and ordained, as the Church struggles to find a language that maintains distinction without falling back into a notion of separation.

---

[19] Jurgen Moltmann, *The Church in the Power of the Spirit* (London 1994), p. 309.
[20] Ibid., p. 308.

In his book *The Life and Work of a Priest*, John Pritchard looks for ways of describing the distinctive work of the ordained as it relates to the corporate ministry:

> It's as if God is the supreme Artist, who invites us into his studio … He promises to be constantly available as tutor, adviser and friend and then he says, 'Let's paint!' Because this is a long-term project he also appoints a few people to act as convenors of the painting workshop, not because they're any better at painting than anyone else but simply because he calls them.[21]

Clearly, this affirms the corporate nature of the ministry; all are painting but some have the functional role of convenors, because God appoints them. The book offers 15 different aspects of a priest's work with a different image for each. While these sections contain useful reflections about the reality of the multifaceted life of a parish priest, they do not offer an integrated picture or any sense of how the variety is managed. This work highlights one of the major problems of a functional model of priesthood: it needs to deal with a role that involves many different tasks and modes of being and is therefore not easily defined. Can the role of a parish priest be reduced to a list of tasks or functions? What does a paint workshop convenor do, and how much is that shaped by the other painters? Returning to Macquarrie's thoughts on ordination, we find that although he stresses the corporate nature of ministry, he argues that a purely functional understanding of a minister, defined by his tasks, is always inadequate. People are more than functional; they develop a character.

> This is surely true of the Christian minister. We can list his various roles and functions – he is servant, proclaimer, priest; he preaches, baptises, presides at the eucharist, and so on … If ministry were merely a role or a function or a collection of functions, then there might seem to be no need for a distinctive ordained ministry in the church. The church would consist, so to speak, of modular Christians, any one of whom might, perhaps at a moment's notice, be fitted into any appropriate functional slot.[22]

He suggests that we need to look at the *character* of the one doing all these things, an aspect that will be developed later in the book. At this point it is important to note that a purely functional definition of the ordained is inadequate. It is not even simply inadequate: it is, in fact, extremely difficult to agree a definition of what a parish priest does. This in turn makes distinguishing the role of clergy from others sharing in the corporate ministry problematic and risks returning to the concept that a priest is merely defined by her liturgical and Eucharistic ministry.

---

[21] John Pritchard, *The Life and Work of a Priest* (London 2007), p. 7.

[22] Macquarrie, *Theology Church and Ministry*, p. 168.

The extreme difficulty of defining the function of clergy is one of the main issues of this book. Towler and Coxon published a sociological study of Anglican clergy in the late 1970s and wrote this:

> Now the clergyman, more than anyone else on the contemporary scene, is a jack of all trades. He occupies a unique position, but the uniqueness of his position has nothing to do with unique skills, or even with unique competence. There is nothing which he does that could not be done equally well by a lawyer or bricklayer in the congregation whom the Bishop had ordained to the Auxiliary Pastoral Ministry. He does not have a job at all in any sense which is readily understandable today, and today, more than ever before, a person must have a job in order to fit into society.[23]

Clergy do not have the same kind of recognisable skills as people in other professions may have. Both within and beyond the Church there seem to be people who can and are doing similar work, albeit not as ordained priests. So how is ordained ministry to be defined? In a functional understanding of ministry there has been a tendency to simply describe the distinctive role of the clergy as leadership. A parish priest is thus to be the church leader. Yet what does this mean? It can, of course, relate straight back to the image of shepherds leading their flocks, though as I noted earlier, this does not answer questions about collaborative ministry.

A large strand of writing for today's clergy looks to leadership models from other professions, drawing on management and strategic leadership ideas from secular writing on leadership theory. It is certainly true that parish priests are running organisations with the requisite need for many to manage staff, paid and voluntary, buildings, budgets and strategic planning. In some of the larger churches the numbers of staff, size of budgets and para-Church organisations can make this a considerable managerial task. It may therefore seem logical to draw on management and leadership thinking from the secular world. Such work can be helpful in thinking about the specifically managerial tasks of some parishes, but leadership in the Church does not have the clarity of structure and purpose that we find in business or other secular models; the relationship is not based on patterns of employment, pay, contracts or productivity. The power structures are far more ambiguous and outcomes much harder to identify and measure. Martyn Percy writes:

> Part of the difficulty for most clergy is that, unlike the conductor of an orchestra, or the CEO of a major corporation, they lack the powerbase to execute decisive initiatives or decisions ... Even the Archbishop of Canterbury is not analogous to being the chairman of a large company ... There is no relationship of

---

[23]   R. Towler and A. Coxon, *The Fate of the Anglican Clergy: A Sociological Study* (London 1979), p. 54. This study followed students from theological college through analysis of their future careers and questionnaires informed by the work of Eysenck and the Allport–Vernon–Lindsey study of values.

compulsion between the leader of the church and the led. Some understanding of this dynamic is important for the study of ministry and its development. Clergy very seldom have the privilege of being strategic; they only have the possibility of being tactical and pragmatic. Moreover, even when they think they are being strategic in leadership, no assumptions can be made about the tactics and pragmatism of the laity in the congregation.[24]

He concludes that clergy can only be 'partially professionalised', for their leadership role is always shaped and defined by the particularity of the community, by the way the community understands the role of the clergy and how much power they are prepared to accord to their vicar.

Percy also comments on how, in the Church, power is fundamentally connected to God; this means that we can find a conflation between the leader and God or, as he puts it, between 'the giver and the gift'.[25] Consequently although the starting point is different, functional models of ministry can, like essentialist models, end by imaging the clergy as more God- or Christ-like than the laity. They often draw on Christological patterns, drawing parallels between Jesus' 'leadership' style and their own. Again we see the valuing of the traditional imagery of shepherd and, currently, the language of 'servant leadership',[26] which subtly aligns leadership to the language of Jesus as Good Shepherd and Servant King.

To summarise the discussion so far, a traditionally Catholic theology – which understands the authority of the ordained proceeding from a moment of origin, in Jesus' commissioning of the Apostles, and a continuity of succession – has led to an essentialist doctrine that sees the ordained priesthood as fundamentally different from the laity. The relationship is then to be understood as complementary: the priest and laity together are the Church and they fulfil their respective roles because of their ontology. The priests' authority is Christ-given and they are to represent Christ to the Church. However, beyond the liturgical roles, who defines what it is to be priestly or lay and is it possible to prevent the former being seen as superior to the latter, particularly being presented as more Christ-like than the laity? On the other hand, an understanding of clergy as emerging out of the needs of the Church is more pragmatic in understanding their role. They are to provide order, leadership and ministry to the Church. However, what exactly this means and how the roles are to be filled is still difficult to define, beyond liturgical and administrative tasks. There is also the increasingly important question of how the ministry of the ordained relates to the ministry of the non-ordained. A purely functional understanding of ministry seems to undermine the need for ordination. Do the clergy define the different roles or the wider church, and what part does God play?

---

[24]   Percy, *Clergy: The Origin of the Species*, p. 166.

[25]   Ibid., p. 113.

[26]   A term borrowed from Robert Greenleaf, www.greenleaf.org.uk which has led to popular courses in the Church of England on developing a 'servant leadership' style of parish ministry.

Chapter 2
Ministry: Relationship and Grace

The previous chapter looked at ontological and functional understandings of ministry and found that both were problematic for understanding a collaborative model of ministry. If we move away from essentialist differences how do we articulate the role of the ordained? Is there a way of speaking meaningfully about the distinctive nature of ordination that does not diminish the reality of the ministry of all? Austin Farrer, writing in the late 1960s, summed up the problem thus:

> There is nothing to stop a layman from being more learned and a more penetrating theologian than the priest of his parish; nothing certainly to prevent a layman from being a much more understanding helper of people in any sort of trouble or sorrow. What distinctive place does (the priest) hold in the mighty purpose of God?[1]

If all share in the priesthood of believers and if many lay people share in the functional tasks of the ordained, what is *distinctive* about the clergy?

A report in 1987 commissioned by the Church of England's advisory body on ministry posed the question 'What Ordained Ministry Does the Church of England Require?'[2] Robin Greenwood comments on this report:

> The document boldly turns on its head much previous understanding of ordination expressed in terms of the individual. Rather, it states that it is the nature of the Church itself that determines the nature of its ministry. It emphasises that ordained ministry should be discussed only in the context of ecclesiology, in that all ministry should be referred to the ministry of Christ in the Church.[3]

The subsequent report, though understanding ministry in this corporate sense, still talked about 'two kinds of ministry', meaning that of universal priesthood and that of the ordained. Yet it tried to find a way of articulating the relationship to affirm the mutuality of a corporate ministry:

> It is not that the clergy have the same kind of responsibilities and ministry as lay people in a more concentrated form. This reduces lay people to a *less*

---

[1]   Austin Farrer, 'Walking Sacraments', in Ann Loades and Robert MacSwain (eds), *The Truth Seeking Heart* (Norwich 2006), pp. 138–41, p. 139.

[2]   Advisory Council for the Church's Mission, 'Education for the Church's Ministry', occasional paper No. 22 (1987), p. 24.

[3]   Robin Greenwood, *Transforming Priesthood* (London 1994), p. 56.

concentrated imitation or replication of the clergy. Rather, the ordained ministry
has a different purpose and responsibility from that of the laity. This involves
ordained ministers in contributing to all the other ministries, by helping to form
and clarify the latter in such a way that the other ministries can exemplify and
sustain the four marks of the Church.[4]

> The particular responsibility of the ordained is to be a means for the church as
> an institution to sustain its living tradition, its responsibility to Christ ... The
> ordained are not the sole means of achieving this but have this particular
> responsibility of holding up to the church its true nature and calling.[5]

The report described the relationship as integral, with the ordained and lay
'interanimating' each other.
    Cocksworth and Brown in *Being a Priest Today* describe this interanimation as
'an intense for-otherness'. They affirm that all Christians share in the ministry of
the Church and that the ordained and the lay are essentially the same:

> Presbyters are not a caste outside the *laos*, they are a category within the *laos*.
> They are members of the *laos*, who are placed in a particular pastoral relation to
> the other members of the *laos* ... presbyters are defined by their relationship to
> other members of the *laos*.[6]

The key point is that it is in the *relationship* that each is defined. The relationship
is a mutual one with two subjects. A priest cannot be a priest except in relationship
with people:

> The presbyter needs the people to be a presbyter. The people need a presbyter to
> be the people of God.[7]

But how can this relationship be articulated in a meaningful way that accepts
distinctions and encourages models of collaboration?

Greenwood's Trinitarian Model

One suggestion for understanding the relationships within the ministry of the
church is to turn to Trinitarian theology, drawing on mutuality and interrelatedness
in the Godhead as a pattern. Greenwood offers a good example of this, utilising the

---

[4]   ABM 1 (1991), p. 32.

[5]   Ibid., p. 34.

[6]   Christopher Cocksworth and Rosalind Brown, *Being a Priest Today* (Norwich
2002), p. 15.

[7]   Ibid., p. 19.

Trinitarian idea of *perichoresis* to expand his understanding of interconnection, mutuality and distinction. He writes:

> The relational Trinitarianism which represents Christian orthodoxy allows the Church to recognise and work with the complexity of God's activity in the world, avoiding inappropriate polarisations and dichotomies, notably between Church and the world and between ordained and non-ordained.[8]

In using a Trinitarian language he aims to define difference while affirming mutuality and interdependence. The clergy role is seen as 'overseeing' in a 'presidential' role, but what matters is the ongoing mutual relationship between the priest and those who accept this oversight. Greenwood's vision of collaborative ministry and his understanding of a relationship that is seeking to avoid patterns of domination but understand necessary asymmetry is a good one. However, there are problems with his use of Trinitarian theology and particularly modelling patterns of relationship on the *perichoresis*, the internal relationship of the Trinity.

Karen Kilby coherently outlines how the concept of *perichoresis*, the internal relationship within the Godhead, relies on the projection of a preconceived model of interrelationship onto the Godhead which is then in turn used to inform human relating:

> In short, then, I am suggesting we have here something like a three-stage process. First a concept, *perichoresis*, is used to name what is not understood, to name whatever it is that makes the three persons one. Secondly, the concept is filled out rather suggestively with notions borrowed from our own experience of relationships and relatedness. And then, finally, it is presented as an exciting resource Christian theology has to offer the wider world in its reflections upon relationships and relatedness.[9]

Thus we see how in Greenwood's case the concept of *perichoresis* is used to give theological significance to ideals of the interrelatedness of ministry. However, because the nature of the mutual relationship within the Godhead is defined by our human understandings of ideal relationships his theology is inevitably shaped by his understanding of good relationships.

Greenwood asserts that his vision is non-hierarchical, but that is because his understanding and concept of the Trinitarian relationship eschews any sense of hierarchy. He is motivated for good reasons to argue for a non-hierarchical, mutually affirming ministry, and his understanding of the Godhead correlates to this vision. However, others may have a more hierarchical understanding of the

---

[8] Greenwood, *Transforming Priesthood*, p. 68.

[9] Karen Kilby, 'Perichoresis and Projection: Problems with Social Doctrines of the Trinity', *New Blackfriars*, 2000, vol. 81, pp. 432–45, p. 443.

Trinity and a different concept of the internal relationship of the Godhead. Thus to liken the priest to the Person of the Father *will* carry with it a sense of hierarchy in less theologically nuanced understandings of the Trinity, conflating the clergy with the central figure of the Godhead. This is not helped by the choice of presiding as his analogy for the priestly role, which connects too easily to concepts of governmental presidents beyond the Church and Eucharistic ministry within it.

It therefore follows that a Trinitarian model of integrated relationship can fall into the same difficulties as Christological models; that is, the clergy begin to seem more like God or Christ than the laity, however much mutuality is stressed. Just as we saw in Christological models, the tensions in holding together complex theological paradoxes can all too easily get mapped on to the tensions inherent in the relationship between the priesthood of the ordained and the priesthood of all. Thus, I would argue, neither a Christological doctrine of representative ministry or a Trinitarian model of integrated ministry seems to provide a coherent language for exploring the interrelationship of the ordained and the laity. Those like Greenwood who have argued for a Trinitarian model are, I suggest, right in arguing that the patterns of ministry need to be understood relationally rather than simply functionally. However, I would maintain they are mistaken in trying to locate the pattern for that relationship in divine rather than human models.

Human Models of Relationship

In order to better articulate the relational nature of ministry I suggest that we move away from the language of leadership which tends to favour hierarchical models and image ministry as a responsive relationship of caring. The language of care is already present in the establishment of the relationship between priest and parish. When each parish priest is inducted or installed by the bishop he uses the phrase 'Receive this cure of souls which is both yours and mine.'[10] The term 'cure' derives from the Latin *cura*. The English word curate to describe a parish priest comes from the same root. In this sense caring and taking charge are about the responsibility of tending to the needs of others, at its best displaying that 'intense for-otherness' that Cocksworth and Brown highlight. It will involve, in certain circumstances, assuming appropriate authority and power, managing both people and resources, as well as planning and implementing strategies, but all of these are to be driven by the relational priority of caring.

The terminology of a caring relationship does not immediately resolve the problem of describing a relationship of mutuality. Caring relationships are often asymmetric, as one has the responsibility of caring for another and reciprocity is not necessarily in kind. In later chapters this question of reciprocity will be explored

---

[10]   These are the words used in a service of induction of an incumbent in the Church of England.

more fully, drawing particularly on Nel Noddings' ethics of caring.[11] At this point I want to suggest that understanding the relationship between the ordained and the wider Church they minister to as a relationship of care can provide a better starting point for exploring the interrelation than the language of leadership. It can also begin to point a way forward to articulating the distinctions.

On one level what I am saying is nothing new. Ministry has traditionally been understood in its widest sense as a form of caring and pastoral work, and carries the imagery of careful tending. Yet, as I argued above, traditional pastoral imagery prioritises the distinction between the priest and those cared for: a shepherd metaphor can and should lead to a genuinely caring pattern of ministry, but the shepherd, at one level, does not see the sheep as like himself. In looking at the language of the priest as one who cares, it is important that the imagery offers a model that maintains the intimacy of the connection between priest and people; the language used needs to convey the sameness as well as the distinctions.

This is why I am arguing for an imagery taken from human relationships, the image of a mother caring for her children. It is an intimate relationship characterised by love and kinship, a relationship that involves responsibility and is constantly adapting to the changing needs and strengths of the children. Both share a common humanity and a common sense of family. A mother is only a mother because she has children to care for and her mothering is dependent on the particularity of the children, who are not static but constantly growing, developing, challenging and rewarding. The rest of this book will explore the metaphor further looking at mothering and ministry and what it might mean for a parish priest to be like a mother tenderly caring.

However, before exploring this maternal imagery it needs to be acknowledged that there is already a language widely used about priesthood based on human patterns of relating and kinship. This is the language of the priest as a father. This language has a long tradition. The father is understood as the head of the family and household, caring and providing for those he loves and is responsible for. In many parts of the Church the priest is simply referred to as Father. The title of Father is particularly associated with traditions where the priest is celibate and is seen to have foregone a family of his own so that he can more adequately focus on the family of Christians entrusted to him. However, the image of father carries very different cultural resonances to that of mother.

In modern Western society ideas of parenting are beginning to change the perception of fathers, but there is still, for many, a legacy of distant, authoritarian and hierarchical models of fatherhood that colour the term. Patriarchal imagery has a problematic history in terms of women's access to authority and it is associated with a privileging of male over female. The use of the term father is also most often associated with churches that have a distinctive view of the priesthood, that do not ordain women and that have a strong view of clerical authority in terms of

---

[11] Nel Noddings, *Caring: A Feminine Approach to Ethics and Moral Education* (Berkeley 1984).

doctrine and practice. For these reasons the language and image of the priest as a father does not primarily indicate a relationship of care. I concede that as patterns of parenting change this may well alter how the term is understood. Yet there is another problem with father language. The language and imagery of father is used extensively to describe and address God. This means that it is all too easy for ideas about God as father and the priest as father to be conflated.

Grace and Sacrament

In arguing for a human metaphor for understanding the role of a parish priest and in eschewing an essentialist view of priesthood, critics may well ask where is God's calling and God's grace? Farrer, whose quote above posed the question 'What distinctive place does (the priest) hold in the mighty purpose of God?', answered it by calling priests 'walking sacraments'.[12] In the last section of this chapter I will explore how we might understand the priest as a walking sacrament within the context of the earlier discussion of ministry. Our starting point is that the ministry clergy are engaged in is not a separate ministry to others in the Church, but is a part of the corporate ministry that all share in. However, through ordination, and through the licensing of the bishop, a parish priest has been put in a particular relationship with a particular community, with responsibility for their spiritual care. The prayer of ordination asks God to send down the Holy Spirit to equip the individual for the work of a priest. How then do we understand the role of grace in the priestly ministry and in the sacraments she is authorised to administer? How does that relate to the concept of a ministry of care? And how does it relate to the corporate ministry? In order to answer these questions I will draw on Karl Rahner's theological ideas on grace and sacraments.

Rahner's Theology of Grace

Rahner's theology of grace arises from his understanding of divine self-communication. In creation and in the person of Christ, God is graciously giving himself to the world, inviting the possibility of relationship. This divine self-communication is experienced as grace and the pinnacle of God's graciousness to humanity is found in Christ. Central to Rahner's understanding of grace is its universality.[13] God's grace is not a rare event but a part of the human condition. It is not poured out on the few, but abundantly.[14] God's grace is present in human relationships in the selfless acts of compassion and kindness that reflect humanity

---

[12]   Farrer, 'Walking Sacraments'.

[13]   Karen Kilby, *Karl Rahner* (London 1997), p. 25.

[14]   Karl Rahner, *Theological Investigations IV*, translated by Kevin Smyth (London 1966), p. 180.

as it was created to be. Such acts are therefore, in some sense, Christ-like. They are, he maintains, 'a concrete manner of actualising love for God'.[15] Such acts can happen in all sorts of ordinary and mundane encounters at moments in which the love for the other enables us to truly reach out to them, forgetting ourselves and focusing on their needs. In such moments and acts of love, God, by grace, is present. This is true even where the concept of grace is not explicit or even intentional on the part of the one acting:

> The Lord himself says that he is present, though, at times, unrecognised, wherever anyone shows compassion from one's heart to another.[16]

Rahner talks about both the reality of this grace and also its fragility. It is not possible to fully discern the motivations and true compassion of human acts and thus not possible to make definitive claims about a specific act being grace-filled. A genuine act of kindness will be grace-filled, but only God can see the truths of our motivation, recognising when we really are genuine. However, the Church traditionally claims that there are acts about which definitive claims can be made. In the formal sacraments of the Church grace is guaranteed. Rahner affirms this guarantee of grace in the sacraments and, as a Roman Catholic, accepts seven formal sacraments. He defends his position by locating the sacraments ecclesiologically. It is because the Church itself is a sacrament, a real symbol of God's grace that the sacraments it recognises and practises are themselves real symbols of grace. Kilby summarises Rahner's position thus:

> The Church itself, he suggests, *is* a sacrament. It is the primary, fundamental sacrament, and the particular sacraments – the sacraments in the usual sense of the word – can be thought of as flowing from, and deriving their meaning from, this basic character of the Church.[17]

Rahner locates the sacraments in the Church because it is 'the body of Christ'. As Kilby explains for Rahner the role of the Church is in 'making grace tangible, of symbolising grace'.[18] The efficacy of the sacraments does not depend on the holiness of the minister, but the holiness of the minister is part of the witness of the Church to its reality as the body of Christ, and this witness is necessary for the meaningful survival of the sacraments. Rahner comments that if none of the ministers of the Church witnessed to the graciousness of God the sacraments would lose their symbolism because people could not recognise them. So witnessing to the reality of God's grace is one of the responsibilities of the clergy.

---

[15]   Ibid., p. 81.
[16]   Jerry Farmer, 'Ministry and Worship', in Declan Marmion and Mary Hines (eds), *The Cambridge Companion to Karl Rahner* (Cambridge 2005), p. 151.
[17]   Kilby, *Karl Rahner*, p. 46.
[18]   Ibid., p. 47.

So how do the formal sacraments differ from the work of grace in human acts of compassion and self-communication? Rahner describes them as 'real symbols' and 'sacramental signs' to express the fact that they do not simply represent a truth but also make that truth present. The sacraments that are recognised by the Church, and enacted by the Church, in explicitly witnessing to the self-communicating grace of God, do more than point to that truth; they also make present the reality of that grace. They are not simply pointers to God's past actions of self-giving, but continual experiences of a gracious self-communication that is ongoing. These formal sacraments bear witness to the ongoing grace of God and the reality of God's presence in the Church and because of that they guarantee the presence of grace. In this they contrast with the impossibility of defining or delineating the gracious self-communication of God which is at work in the acts of love present in human moments of self-giving. The Church and its sacraments are necessary witnesses and guarantees of God's graciousness that can help communities and individuals recognise and receive the grace that is always on offer.

As an Anglican I am not bound by a tradition of seven formal sacraments and I do not follow Rahner's commitment on this point. However, what I find particularly interesting is his theory of sacraments arising out of the sacramental nature of the Church. As I have argued above, the ministry of the ordained arises out of and is part of the corporate ministry of the Church. The act of ordination authorises an individual to be a recognised minister and to bear explicit witness to the love of God as understood in the Christian faith. The authority ministers are given involves both a role in the formal sacraments of a given denomination and a wider ministry of pastoral care. In the former the role is quite clearly delineated. For example, the sacraments of baptism and the Eucharist are shaped by the authorised rituals and symbols which themselves make the acts sacramental; God's grace is manifested and offered in tangible forms – holy water, bread blessed and broken – which are received literally and by faith. The priest's role in such sacraments is clearly defined and, in a sense, simply needs to be enacted. Apart from basic training in how to conduct the appropriate services, using the accepted words and actions, the priest does not need any great skill to play her part in such sacramental ministry, though her recognised authority is intrinsic to the meaning.

However, in order for the sacraments to be *recognised* as the grace of God the wider ministry of the Church and its representatives needs to witness to the graciousness of God. In the wider aspects of ministry, especially in pastoral care, the priest needs to rely on the same abilities as any Christian to act compassionately, seeking to love God and neighbour, bearing witness to God's reconciling love in Christ. As I will explore in later chapters, such acts of compassion are concrete and contingent so cannot be subject to a formulaic approach. Rahner comments on the way that changes in the world bring new situations where the Church has to reflect on what it means to respond graciously.[19] Yet, because of a priest's authorised role

---

[19]   He notes that the Church is constantly surprised by new situations, 'tasks which it has simply never preached from the pulpit in the "good old days" – tasks whose moment

to represent the Church, this wider ministry is also in some sense sacramental because the actions of the priest are received as symbolic of the actions of the Church, and thus of God. When a priest speaks words of forgiveness or blessing, offers comfort or a challenge, even when these are not said in a ritual setting, the words she says will be received not simply as her own words but as the word of the Church and, at some level, the word of God. This is part of the responsibility of ordination. The priest, in showing such acts of compassion, is like any other human being, yet through the authority of ordination she has the responsibility to name the transformative work of grace as the work of Christ so that it can be recognised as such.

It is not possible to provide a formulaic account of the sacramental nature of the priest's ministry in this general sense; it cannot be pinned to any particular tasks or functions of the priest's work. The grace that flows in and through priestly ministry is not different from the grace that flows through all human acts of compassion and goodness. It therefore follows that the ministerial acts of a priest, aside from the particular roles undertaken in the formal sacraments, are in essence the same kinds of acts of compassion and caring that should be part of all Christian lives and any good life. It is all the same ministry and the priest will herself receive grace through the acts of compassion and love of others within and beyond their congregation; a fact that most clergy would testify to.

In my understanding, ordination confers on an individual the responsibility of bearing witness to the nature of the Church and caring for particular communities, helping them to grow in their ability to act graciously and witness to the graciousness of God. In order for the priest to witness effectively to the grace of God, the Church's ministry must be effective, which means that the individuals who make up the Church need to learn how to live and act in accordance with God's compassion and to bear witness to his reconciling love. God's grace is not dependent on the holiness of individuals, but the ongoing witness to that grace is a necessary part of the ability of others to participate in the reception of grace. It therefore follows that all Christians need to develop the capacity to act in loving and compassionate ways. They also need to be able to reflect on how such actions bear witness to God's love and graciousness. The ordained have a particular responsibility for reflecting on such behaviour and articulating the graciousness of God so that their own acts, the acts of the Church and the wider acts of goodness in the world can be understood as manifestations of God's love.

What is important to note at this point is that because grace is dependent on the free gift of God, no individual can quantify or control grace. Its flow is, in a sense, a mystery. To borrow a maternal image, it is like breastfeeding, in which the mother participates by offering herself to the child but has no actual control of how much milk she is producing or the child receiving. The needs of the baby stimulate the flow of milk, and the type of milk received. The mother cannot determine

for Christianity has come but slowly to Christian consciousness'. Karl Rahner, *The Love of Jesus and the Love of Neighbour* (Slough 1983), p. 73.

quantities; she can only fully know that the child is being well fed by looking for the signs of health and contentment in the baby. Even though I have argued that the grace can be, as Rahner puts it, guaranteed in sacramental acts, in the wider ministry all that clergy can do is offer themselves as bearers of God's love and compassion. How God's grace flows through these encounters and the way that the grace is received is a mystery that is firmly in God's hands. Yet where there are signs of transformation and of spiritual growth we can know that God's grace is flowing and being received. Therefore clergy need to learn to look for the signs of flourishing in the people they minister to.

The ministry is the ministry of the Church and it is God's ministry. The individuals who take on the responsibility of ordination can be seen as 'walking sacraments'. They are not simply appointed by the members of a church, as a purely functional understanding of their role might suggest but, at some level, chosen and equipped by God. Yet this sense of vocation is most often mediated through the community of the Church, through affirmations of an individual's ability to communicate and witness to the love of God. It is also tested by the wider Church with the assumption that God's will is discerned through human criteria that makes reasoned judgements about an individual's capacity to bear witness in this particular way to the grace of God at work in the world. This is not to diminish the work of the Holy Spirit, but to affirm the corporate nature of the Church in which and through which the Spirit works, in which and through which the ministry of Christ is made manifest. Grace is experienced in and through the relationships we have with others.

When individuals are authorised by the Church through ordination to take on the role of a priest, they need to learn in relationship with the wider Church how to live out that calling. If, as we have concluded above, the clergy need to hone their human skills of kindness and compassion in order to minister and bear witness to the gracious work of God, it follows that we can learn about ministry through drawing on human relationships of care. It also seems appropriate to draw on the relationship in which most people first experience care and begin to learn how to care themselves; mothering. Thus I am offering a maternal metaphor to help explore the role of a parish priest. Like any model, it has its limitations. Yet I maintain that it can offer new insights and a rich imagery that can help articulate the role of a priest who has accepted the 'cure of souls' and seeks to live out the responsibility of the relationship carefully.

Chapter 3
Maternal Imagery for Clergy in the Christian Tradition

In choosing to use a maternal model for ministry I am moving away from familiar images, but not suggesting a totally new language. Maternal metaphors, while not central to the tradition, have been used before. As this is not a dominant tradition, I am particularly grateful to the scholars and interest groups who have brought examples of maternal imagery to light. I am interested in exploring ways in which mothering has been related to the ministry of priests and abbots. There is an important body of work that looks at how maternal imagery in the Bible relates to the divine and how maternal metaphors can enhance our understanding of God. These theologians have offered important insights into the language the church uses to explore God and how we do, or do not, value maternal metaphors.[1] Whilst I acknowledge how language about God and the imagery used can often impact on the way clergy are perceived, this chapter will not explore imagery of the divine but focus on maternal metaphors and images specifically linked to the work of one who is a recognised minister in the Church.

It is also important to acknowledge that within the Christian tradition, language about motherhood is most often used in relation to the Virgin Mary. However, it is not within the scope of this book to explore Marian imagery in any detail. I will though explore strands of the tradition that have seen her as a model for priests, or as a prototype priest. As will become clear, the examples explored in this chapter refer to male clergy and do not make any correlation between maternal imagery and a suggestion that women could or should fulfil the same role.

The church has historically restricted priesthood as a role for men. Thus imagery about church leadership roles has principally assumed that they are held by men. Yet there is a tradition of women in positions of leadership within the Church, not as priests but as leaders of religious orders where maternal language has been utilised. The title of 'Mother' has been and in many cases continues to be routinely used for women in such positions. It seems most likely that this

---

[1]   For example: Sallie McFague, *Metaphorical Theology: Models of God in Religious Language* (London 1983); Phyllis Trible, *God and the Rhetoric of Sexuality* (London 1978); Elizabeth Johnson, *She Who Is: The Mystery of God in Feminist Theological Discourse* (New York 1999). Maternal imagery has also been important in aspects of spiritual writing. Julian of Norwich used maternal language to speak of Jesus in the fourteenth century in *The Revelations of Divine Love*. More recently, Janet Morley's prayers and reflections collected in *All Desires Known* (London 1988) offer examples of using maternal imagery for God.

was simply a feminine version of the male title of father rather than a deliberate attempt to understand the role as being mother-like. However, without any serious historical examination of the use of the title it is hard to know how important the maternal imagery was to those who used it.

This chapter is inevitably sketchy, because there is no systematic study of maternal imagery associated with the clergy role. Some aspects are better researched than others. Caroline Walker Bynum's work on the Cistercians is scholarly and detailed.[2] As is Gaventa's work on St Paul. However, the language of Mother Church is far more diffuse and the limits on my exploration of it in this chapter are a reflection on the limited literature that explores the concept. There is much more work to be done on exploring this maternal imagery but in this chapter I am simply highlighting that it is not a new thing to suggest that in some ways ministry is like mothering. Recovering some of the historical imagery, however marginal, can provide a foundation for exploring the imagery further in modern understandings of ministry.

St Paul: Like a Mother

The New Testament offers a few examples of maternal imagery to talk about the work of ministry. These come from St Paul's description of his own apostolic work. The clearest example of this is in the first letter to the Thessalonians:

> But we were gentle among you, like a nurse taking care of her children. So, being affectionately desirous of you, we were ready to share with you not only the gospel of God but also our own selves, because you had become very dear to us.[3]

In modern English the full imagery of this text is often lost because we do not commonly use the term nursing for breastfeeding. Commentators note that it is a nurse caring for her *own* children.[4] In this verse Paul likens his ministry to a mother breastfeeding her children and he goes on in the following verse to explore the metaphor. He stresses the affection in which the Thessalonians were held and the fact that in his ministry amongst them, he shared not simply the message of the gospel but himself, through a form of self-giving motivated by loving involvement. The image of a woman breastfeeding a child provides a strong picture of affectionate involvement and self-giving. As Best notes in his commentary on the passage:

---

2   Caroline Walker Bynum, *Jesus as Mother* (Berkeley 1982).

3   1 Thessalonians 2:7–8, RSV.

4   Ernest Best, *A Commentary on First and Second Thessalonians* (London 1972), p. 102.

We have a somewhat unusual picture of ministerial care, more tender than that of pastor or shepherd.[5]

He also quotes Calvin's comments on this passage:

> A mother in nursing her child makes no show of authority and does not stand on dignity … (and) reveals a wonderful and extraordinary love, because one spares no trouble or effort, avoids no care, is wearied by their coming and going, and gladly even gives her own life to be drained.[6]

The mother holds her child and the necessary nourishment flows from one to the other. It provides an image of ministry that is nurturing and tender, a ministry that requires time and attachment. Beverley Gaventa comments that the Greek verb *thalpein* is used, which means to warm, cherish, comfort.[7]

Gaventa goes on to argue that this is not Paul's only use of breastfeeding imagery. In the first letter to the Corinthians he talks about feeding them with milk:

> But I, brethren, could not address you as spiritual men, but as men of the flesh, as babes in Christ. I fed you with milk, not solid food; for you were not ready for it; and even yet you are not ready, for you are still of the flesh.[8]

Commentators have often connected this passage to philosophical debates about milk and solids but Gaventa draws attention to the fact that Paul speaks of himself as the one who supplies the milk. The only way for milk to be properly supplied to babies is through the process of breastfeeding. She notes that the idea of Paul as the one who feeds distinguishes his use of the imagery from that of other Hellenistic philosophers:

> Paul does not speak with Philo's detachment about what food the soul requires or about the 'shape of instruction'. Neither does Paul cajole the Corinthians to cease their crying 'for mothers and nurses'. Instead, he images himself as the mother who nurtures, the one who knows what food is appropriate for her children. In other words, even though the image of milk and meat was current, Paul does something distinctive with it: he presents himself as the mother of the Corinthians … And the language is unequivocal: Paul is the nursing mother of the Church.[9]

---

[5]   Ibid., p. 102.

[6]   Cited in ibid., p. 102 from J. Calvin, *The Epistle of Paul the Apostle to the Romans and to the Thessalonians*, translated by Ross Mackenzie (Edinburgh, 1961).

[7]   Beverly Gaventa, *Our Mother St Paul* (Louisville 2007).

[8]   1 Corinthians 3:1–3a, RSV.

[9]   Gaventa, *Our Mother St Paul*, p. 45.

It is not only breastfeeding imagery that Paul uses, but also the labouring of childbirth. In Galatians he uses a rather complex metaphor:

> My little children, with whom I am again in travail until Christ be formed in you.[10]

The Greek word used for 'travail', *odinein*, refers to the physical process of childbirth, including its accompanying pains. Here Paul seems to stress his involvement with the people he is ministering to. Using imagery that is both maternal and physical, he underlines the depth of his commitment to these people and the desire that this will lead to new life. Gaventa argues that Paul uses maternal imagery to highlight the ongoing relationship necessary for nurturing Christian faith. She contrasts the way Paul uses maternal and paternal images:

> Maternal imagery appears in contexts referring to the ongoing nature of the relationship between Paul and the congregations he founded; paternal imagery, by contrast, regularly refers to the initial stage of Christian preaching and conversion.[11]

Thus we can see the contrast between an episodic relation – founding a church or making a convert – and the ongoing work of relationship involved in nurturing and strengthening a developing community.

Gaventa also argues that Paul was deliberately using metaphors that subverted ideas of hierarchy and authority, referring to himself with maternal images that seem shamefully inadequate for a male leader,[12] just as he frequently used the subversive image of himself as a slave. Paul's use of such maternal imagery is a minor aspect of his writing, but it is interesting to note that at times he turned to the nursing mother or the woman struggling in childbirth in order to convey something about the involved, nurturing care that was one aspect of his understanding of ministry. He was comfortable in using a specifically female image.

Prelates and Abbots as Mother

As we will see from the other examples of this language, maternal imagery is often employed to stress the ongoing nurturing role and is at times used to complement male imagery. A good example of this is the work of Pope Gregory, who wrote a document about ministry in the early seventh century. This work, known as the *Pastoral Care*, utilised many different metaphors to explore the role of the clergy

---

[10]   Galatians 4:19, RSV.

[11]   Gaventa, *Our Mother St Paul*, p. 6.

[12]   Ibid., p. 14.

in their pastoral ministry. We find a maternal image used to stress the importance of gentleness in aspects of pastoral care:

> But let those who are set over others shew themselves such that those who are under them may not blush to make known to them also their secret doings; that, when the little ones endure the buffets of temptation, they may run to the pastor's heart as to their mother's bosom, and wash away, by the comfort of his exhortation and the tears of prayer, that wherein they see themselves beforehand to be polluted by the filth of sin that importuneth them.[13]

This is clearly an encouragement to those in a position of spiritual leadership to be mother-like in their ability to comfort with compassion and tenderness. Further on he shows how maternal and paternal images need to be balanced in the work of Christian leadership:

> For care is to be taken that a ruler should be exhibited to his subjects both as a mother by kindness and a father by discipline.[14]

In using such imagery Gregory is seeking to say something about the quality of care that those with pastoral authority should exhibit. The imagery of a mother offered a recognisable metaphor for comforting involvement, kindness and nurture. The reference is one among many images and I would not wish to imply that it was a particularly prominent image for Gregory; I simply note that it was one he felt comfortable applying to the work of a male Christian leader. It conveyed particular notions about compassion and kindness.

Writing in the eleventh century, Anselm of Canterbury draws on St Paul's maternal imagery both in terms of feeding and birthing. He connects this imagery to the importance of educating people in the faith:

> You [Paul] are among Christians like a nurse who not only cares for her children but also gives birth to them a second time by the solicitude of her marvellous love … Gentle nurse, gentle mother, who are these sons to whom you give birth and nurture if not those whom you bear and educate in the faith of Christ by your teaching?

> … O mother of well known tenderness, may your son feel your heart of maternal piety.[15]

---

[13] Pope Gregory I, *S. Gregory on the Pastoral Charge: The Benedictine Text*, translated by Henry Ramsden Bramley (Oxford 1908), p. 73.

[14] Ibid., p. 87.

[15] Anselm, Prayer 10 to St Paul quoted in Walker Bynum, *Jesus as Mother*, p. 114.

In this meditative prayer Anselm focuses on how Paul is a mother to him and how in the same way Jesus is a mother. Yet both are also fathers and again we see the two types of imagery used to provide a rich balance:

> Both of you are therefore mothers ... For you accomplished, one through the other, and one through himself that we, born to die, may be reborn to life. Fathers you are then by result, mothers by affection; fathers by authority, mothers by kindness; fathers by protection, mothers by compassion. You [Lord] are a mother and you [Paul] are also. Unequal by extent of love, you do not differ in quality of love.[16]

This is a prayer and focuses on how Anselm relates to both Jesus and St Paul. It does not tell us if Anselm drew any parallels between his own roles as a minister with this imagery. However, it is interesting to note the way that the nurturing mother is connected to the 'education in faith' and again, in the second quote, how maternal imagery is used alongside paternal imagery to provide a more rounded image of the pastoral role.

St Paul's metaphor of the nursing mother also seems to have been influential in the writings of Bernard of Clairvaux and a number of other Cistercians in the twelfth century. Walker Bynum in her book *Jesus as Mother* reflects on the maternal language that these monks used, particularly to talk about their role as abbots. In an extract from a letter we see Bernard using a nursing image for his nurturing work with a young monk:

> I begot you in religion by word and example. I nourished you with milk when, while yet a child, it was all you could take ... But alas! How soon and how early you were weaned.[17]

And more explicitly in an extract from a sermon, we see Bernard offering a maternal analogy to help others reflect on their pastoral role:

> Learn that you must be mothers to those in your care, not masters; make an effort to arouse the response of love, not that of fear; and should there be occasional need for severity, let it be paternal rather than tyrannical. Show affection as a mother would, correct like a father. Be gentle, avoid harshness, do not resort to blows, expose your breasts: let your bosom expand with milk not swell with passion ... Why will the young man bitten by the serpent, shy away from the judgement of the priest, to whom he ought rather to run as to the bosom of a mother? If you are spiritual, instruct him in a spirit of gentleness.[18]

---

[16]   Ibid., p. 114.

[17]   Bernard of Clairvaux cited in Walker Bynum, *Jesus as Mother*, p. 117.

[18]   Ibid., p. 118.

Again we see the pairing of maternal and paternal characteristics, yet here we see an expanded imagery about the maternal breast, which is both for feeding and for comfort.

Walker Bynum puts Bernard's writings in context. She notes that in medieval writing maternal language conveyed three basic images. Mothers are generative and sacrificial in giving birth, mothers are loving and tender towards their children and mothers are nurturing, feeding the child from their own body. She comments that this was a period where mothers were strongly encouraged to feed their own children rather than use wet nurses. There was a physiological understanding at the time of breast milk being made from the mother's blood. This physiological understanding, coupled with the knowledge that breastfeeding was necessary for survival and health, fed into imagery of Jesus as a mother feeding his people from his own flesh and blood.[19] For Bernard breasts were a symbol of self-giving, nurturing care and he reflected both on those who nurtured him, including Jesus, and on how leaders should nurture in turn those they cared for. Walker Bynum notes that Bernard used maternal imagery 'to describe Jesus, Moses, Peter, Paul, prelates in general, abbots in general, and, more frequently, himself as abbot'.[20] She comments in particular on the nursing metaphor:

> Breasts to Bernard, are a symbol of the pouring out towards others of affectivity or of instruction and almost invariably suggest to him a discussion of the duties of prelates or abbots. Bernard not only develops an elaborate picture of the abbot (he usually has himself in mind) as mother, contrasting *mater* to *magister* or *dominus* and stating repeatedly that a mother is one who cannot fail to love her child; he also frequently attributes maternal characteristics, especially suckling with milk, to the abbot when he refers to him as father.[21]

Bernard was not alone in using maternal imagery to describe the role of the abbot or prelate. Walker Bynum discusses the writings of Aelred of Rievaulx, Guerric of Igny, Isaac of Stella, Adam of Perseigne, Helinand of Froidmont and William of St Thierry. Aelred's dying words to his monks are reported as, 'I love you all … as earnestly as a mother does her sons.' Bynum writes, 'Aelred, like other Cistercian authors, moves naturally from a discussion of parents and nursing to a discussion of the heavy burdens borne by religious leaders.'[22] She points out that the Cistercians using this imagery were abbots and often novice masters as well, and that the language points to some ambivalence in their attitude to their leadership position. Just as Gaventa saw Paul's use of this imagery as a way of

---

[19]   The imagery around Jesus as a mother feeding his people from his blood can be seen in the use of the pelican feeding her chicks as a representation of Christ. The pelican was believed to feed her young on her own blood, piercing herself in order for the blood to flow.

[20]   Walker Bynum, *Jesus as Mother*, p. 115.

[21]   Ibid., p. 116.

[22]   Ibid., p. 123.

adding a dimension to his understanding of his apostleship, so these abbots used maternal imagery to add the dimension of nurturing to their general conception of leadership. Bynum Walker comments:

> Cistercian abbots were in fact increasingly called upon to respond with qualities that medieval men considered feminine. Anxious, even guilty about ruling, these religious leaders tried to create a new image of authority (both their own and God's) that would temper that authority with compassion and 'mothering'.[23]

Furthermore, she notes the particular thinking about community that was part of the Cistercian movement. There was an emphasis on dependence and interdependence within a community – 'an interdependence in which all are servants and learners'. She maintains that the use of maternal imagery arises out of the need to articulate this dependence and interdependence, which was shaped by love:

> The Cistercian conception of Jesus as mother and abbot as mother reveals not an attitude toward women but a sense (not without ambivalence) of a need and obligation to nurture other men, a need and obligation to achieve intimate dependence on God.[24]

Although women in religious life during this period also used maternal imagery about Jesus, they did not use this language to discuss ideas of the role of a leader. The imagery is used in spiritual meditations on Christ and his relationship with the believer. These women were not in a position to be priests or prelates; they were not, for the most part, even abbesses, though they often offered spiritual advice.[25] Thus their maternal imagery is less connected to ideas of leadership. It is male leaders who utilise mothering language to supplement authority with nurture and harshness with affection.

The work of Walker Bynum has made the Cistercian use of maternal imagery accessible and it is much harder to discover whether it has played a part in enriching the imagery around pastoral leadership in other communities. She does not comment on the use of the title 'mother' by female abbesses and other leaders of religious orders. It does not appear to have been a subject for written reflection, so it is hard to know whether the women who took on the title of mother, in taking responsibility for a particular community, consciously drew on maternal imagery in fulfilling their leadership role. The title of *mater monasterii* or *mater monachorum* appears to have been the accepted term for the leader of the earliest female religious communities.[26] Later many used the title of abbess, but the abbess

---

23   Ibid., p. 158; see also footnote 159.

24   Ibid., p. 168.

25   See Julian of Norwich *Revelations of Divine Love*.

26   Margaret Schaus, *Women and Gender in Medieval Europe: An Encyclopaedia* (London 2006) See the entry for abbesses.

would still be known as 'mother'. Clearly, these spiritual mothers, although not authorised to any priestly sacramental duties, were engaged in pastoral oversight of Christian communities:

> The abbess exercised supreme domestic authority not only over the nuns of the community, but also over the canons or priest living there, the servants and all the families of the monastery's dependencies ... The abbess was responsible for the mundane welfare of the women whose care was entrusted to her and also for their eternal salvation.[27]

It has not been possible to find any commentary about the use of the title 'mother' for women engaged in this role, which the historian Margaret Strauss in her encyclopaedia of medieval women, calls 'a kind of female father with paternal rights'. It is most likely that it was simply both a term of respect and a female equivalent of 'father'. Yet it is interesting to note that this was a widely used title to refer to women engaged in Christian leadership, managing communities, nurturing and educating those in their care and often offering wider spiritual advice. Consciously or unconsciously the title must have had some resonance with cultural ideas about actual motherhood, though of course those who carried the title had foregone the opportunity to give birth and nurse themselves.

Mary: Mother and Priest?

The image of mother within Christian thinking would not only resonate with understandings, usually idealised, about maternal love. They would also resonate with imagery associated with the Holy Mother, Mary the mother of Jesus. It is not possible in the limits of this book to explore the rich imagery that surrounds the figure of Mary. However, there are two aspects of Marian imagery that I wish to note. The first is, like the discussions above, a minor aspect of the tradition that has been highlighted by a particular interest group. This is a history of devotion to Mary as a prototype priest. The second is part of mainstream tradition and this is the association of Mary with the Church, which links to the maternal imagery of Mother Church.

For the idea of Mary as a priest I am indebted to the work of the Campaign for the Ordination of Women in the Catholic Church.[28] This organisation has highlighted what it calls the latent tradition of honouring Mary as a priest. Their website holds a collection of devotional and theological writings on the subject. It is also includes extant images that show Mary wearing a bishop's pallium or a priest's chasuble and stole. These date from the sixth century onwards. The

---

[27] Ibid.

[28] www.womenpriests.org (12 February 2011).

popularity of such images must have continued into the twentieth century because in 1916 Pope Benedict XV banned them:

> After mature examination the Eminent Cardinals, general inquisitors of the Holy Office, have decided that images of the Blessed Virgin Mary wearing priestly vestments are not approved.[29]

His successor, Pope Pius XI, reiterated the position on devotion to Mary as a priest in response to an article in 1927:

> An article on 'The true devotion to the Virgin Priest' that appeared in the *Palestra del Clero de Rovigo* (vol. 6, pp. 71ss) has come to the attention of the Sacred Congregation of the Holy Office. On this subject, the same Sacred Congregation has ordered that your Excellence must draw the attention of the editor of the periodical to this article and warn him that the devotion concerned is not approved and may not be promoted, in conformity with the decree of the Holy Office of the 8th of April 1916.[30]

The timing of the ban is perhaps connected to changes in other Christian denominations. In the early twentieth century women were being admitted to ordained or authorised ministry in a number of denominations while in others the question was being raised. This may have been the reason for the Vatican suppressing a devotion that envisioned any kind of female priest, however exceptional the priesthood of Mary was seen to be.

The references to Mary as priest that have been translated and collected by the campaign group for Women priests in the Roman Catholic church show that her priestly identity is evident in her bringing Christ to birth in the flesh and in offering him both in the temple and ultimately at the cross. One example shows this sense of Mary as the priest:

> Mary is no stranger in anything that belongs to the Eucharist. She was the first priest to call down the Word from heaven to earth and to bring forth Jesus Christ in this world through an act of her will. Therefore she has been called Virgin Priest, *Virgo Sacerdos* ... Just as she has been the first priest to bring forth Jesus Christ, she will be the first priest to offer him. She was the first sacrificer as she had been the first consecrator ... On top of the holy mount of Calvary, she stays upright in the posture of a sacrificer standing before the altar, that is: the cross, where the first Mass is celebrated and where our redemption was

---

[29]   *Acta Apostolicae Sedis* 8 (1916), p. 146, quoted on www.womenpriests.org (12 February 2011).

[30]   Quoted on www.womenpriests.org (12 February 2011).

accomplished … The Virgin Priest who has given us the Eucharist, the Virgin Sacrificer who has validated Mass for us, is also the Virgin of holy communion.[31]

Although Mary's motherhood shapes these aspects of her priestly image, especially her ability to make 'the word' flesh, beyond this her motherhood is relevant only in the sense that it heightens the depth of her sacrificial love. This devotion is primarily focused on the role of the priest in the Eucharist, in a moment of transformation for the elements. It is thus focused on a sacrificial event rather than an ongoing pastoral relationship. In this way it contrasts to the examples we have been looking at before. Here the imagery is about episodic moments in Mary's life when she offers Christ to the world. Attention is drawn to Christ's birth, his being offered in the Temple and his crucifixion and Mary's role in each of these occasions. These sacrificial moments resonate with a priestly theology that is rooted in offering the sacrifice of the mass. Thus, although the devotion to Mary as a priest or as a model for priests is rooted in her motherhood, it does not draw on the ongoing nurturing role of a mother.

Where Mary's ongoing role as a nurturing mother is used, it is more likely to be connected to Mary as a prototype of the Church, which itself is described as the mother of its members, rather than as a prototype priest. It is important to note that the devotion to Mary as priest was not offered as an argument for ordaining women; her unique relationship to Christ makes her an exception. Tina Beattie, however, suggests that this devotional tradition may in fact offer an interesting theological perspective on ordaining women as priests; the possibility of understanding sacrifice as leading to birth and not simply death.[32]

Mother Church

If we turn from Eucharistic imagery to the ongoing life of the Church then we find that maternal language is used of the Church and especially the laity rather than the clergy. This maternal Church is often linked to Marian imagery, but we find that it is not confined to Marian theology. Henri de Lubac sets out to trace the tradition in *The Motherhood of the Church*.[33] He notes how the term 'mother' is used of the Church in the patristic period to describe how Christians are both born and nourished.

---

[31]   Bishop Morelle, *Troisième congrès marial breton* (Saint-Brieuc 1911), pp. xiv–xvi, quoted on www.womenpriests.org (12 February 2011).

[32]   Tina Beattie, *The Month* 257 (December 1996), pp. 485–93, quoted on www. womenpriests.org. See also Ali Green, *A Theology of Women's Priesthood* (London 2009). Green looks extensively at the symbolism of a female priest celebrating the Eucharist.

[33]   Henri de Lubac, *The Motherhood of the Church* (San Francisco 1982).

We are born from her womb, nourished by her milk, animated by her spirit.[34]

The Church is a mother for us … It is from her that we are born spiritually.[35]

On occasions this motherhood is linked to the motherhood of Mary:

Who has given birth to you? I hear the voice of your heart: it is the Mother Church, this holy, honoured Church who, like Mary, gives birth and is virgin … If the one gave birth to the only son, the other gives birth to numerous sons who, by this only son, are gathered into one.[36]

De Lubac goes on to show how the maternal imagery of the Church is linked to its educational role. He quotes Delahaye:

For Hippolytus, the Church is a mother through the transmission of baptism. For Tertullian, she is again mother in her care to educate afterwards.[37]

He also notes the complexity of the analogy in which Mother Church is constantly giving birth, but this birth does not necessarily expel her children from her womb. He quotes Irenaeus:

One must cling to the Church, be brought up within her womb and feed there on the Lord's Scripture.[38]

So the Church as mother is both birthing her children and nurturing them, whether by holding them in her womb or by nursing them with spiritual food.

The language of Mother Church, though now most closely associated with Catholic and Orthodox theology, is also present in the writings of Luther and Calvin. In a sermon of 1528, Luther, reflecting on the Lord's Prayer, states:

The Christian church is your mother, who gives birth to you and bears you through the Word. And this is done by the Holy Spirit, who bears witness concerning Christ.[39]

---

[34]   Cyprian De Ecclesiae catholicae unitate c 5 (Hartel 1:214), cited in de Lubac, *The Motherhood of the Church*, p. 48.

[35]   Augustine, cited in ibid., p. 50.

[36]   Augustine, cited in ibid., p. 57.

[37]   de Lubac, *The Motherhood of the Church*, p. 62.

[38]   Ibid., p. 69.

[39]   Jaroslav Pelikan and Helmut T. Lehmann (eds), *Luther's Works* (St Louis and Philadelphia 1955–72), p. 166.

In the *Institutes* Calvin draws on the patristic imagery of Mother Church, birthing and nurturing the faithful:

> I shall start, then, with the church, into whose bosom God is pleased to gather his sons, not only that they may be nourished by her help and ministry as long as they are infants and children, but also that they may be guided by her motherly care until they mature and at last reach the goal of faith.
>
> …
>
> But because it is now our intention to discuss the visible church, let us learn even from the simple title 'mother' how useful, indeed how necessary, it is that we should know her. For there is no other way to enter into life unless this mother conceive us in her womb, give us birth, nourish us at her breast, and lastly, unless she keep us under her care and guidance until, putting off mortal flesh, we become like the angels. Our weakness does not allow us to be dismissed from her school until we have been pupils all our lives. Furthermore, away from her bosom one cannot hope for any forgiveness of sins or any salvation, as Isaiah and Joel testify.[40]

It is perhaps due to the way that Marian theology and the idea of Mother Church have become intimately connected in much theological writing, that despite Luther and Calvin's acceptance of the term, it is not a feature of current Protestant ecclesiology.

In Anglican theology we see examples of maternal imagery for the Church in the Tractarian movement. A tract published in 1838 by an anonymous author is titled: *The Church of England the Nursing Mother of her People*.[41] The tract describes how throughout an individual's life the Church is there to administer the necessary sacraments or offices to nurture and sustain the 'child'. Yet this imagery of the maternal Church is increasingly connected to a definitively male clergy. It seems that the motherhood of the Church depends not only on the fatherhood of God but also on an exclusively male clergy who symbolise that fatherhood. De Lubac makes this very clear following the chapter in his book entitled 'Motherhood of the Entire Church' with 'Fatherhood of the Clergy':

> It is always owing to the immediate mediation of pastors that this maternal function of all and of each one can be exercised, whether in relation to the Word of God in the individual soul or with regard to the community as a whole.[42]

---

[40]   *John Calvin Works and Correspondence* (electronic edn) (Charlottesville 2002), pp. 1012–16.

[41]   *The Church of England Nursing Mother of her People* (London 1838).

[42]   de Lubac, *The Motherhood of the Church*, p. 85.

As I noted in the previous chapter, this thinking is connected to a theology of ordination in which the priest is essentially different in his priesthood from the common ministry of the Church. The pastors as 'fathers' continue the apostolic tradition. The Apostles 'begot sons' through the preaching of the Gospel and the current clergy take on from them the paternal role of leadership. Commenting on Vatican II de Lubac writes:

> Here again we observe the coincidence between the teaching of the ancient Fathers and that of the last Council. Both establish the same relationship, although sometimes with different words, between the motherhood of the whole Church and the fatherhood of those who receive the mission of directing her ... Those who are called to exercise this 'pastoral' ministry have a share in the responsibility of Christ, the unique Mediator.[43]

This language can become quite complex as the Church, which contains men and women, is described in feminine language as Mother and Bride while the clergy, who are at the same time both part of this maternal Church and symbolically father/bridegroom representing Christ, must be male.

Conclusion

It follows that imagery about the Church as a mother, nurturing and feeding her children, does not lead to maternal language to describe those leading Church communities. The masculinity of priesthood is underpinned by the clergy being understood as *other* to the wider Church in both origin and ongoing relationship. This otherness is then expressed as masculine, in contrast to the Church and ordinary believers being feminine. Yet it does seem strange that the work of the Church can be described as birthing, nurturing, feeding, educating and comforting like a mother but the people who embody this by dispensing spiritual food and teaching in word and sacrament, offering spiritual comfort in pastoral care and absolution are not seen as mother-like. Mary Daly comments ironically on the feminine roles of masculine priests in her article 'The Looking-glass Society':

> Recognising the ineptitude of females in performing even the humble 'feminine' tasks assigned to them by the Divine Plan, the Looking-glass priests raised these functions to the supernatural level in which they alone had competence. Feeding was elevated to become Holy Communion. Washing achieved dignity in Baptism and Penance ... These anointed Male Mothers, who naturally are called Fathers, felt maternal concern for the women entrusted to their pastoral care.[44]

---

[43]   Ibid., p. 93.

[44]   Mary Daly, 'The Looking-Glass Society', in Ann Loades (ed.), *Feminist Theology: A Reader* (Louisville 1990), pp. 189–92, p. 190.

As women have begun to play more significant roles in leadership in wider society and in some areas of the Church, they themselves have shown ambivalence to maternal language. Although some female priests in the Catholic wing of the Anglican Church use the term Mother in the way their male colleagues use Father, this has by no means become standard. It has even been dropped as a title in some female religious orders as they try to explore different patterns of leadership from those of the past. Women do not want to be defined or limited to motherhood for reasons that I will explore in the next chapter. Yet it is a rich image that in the past has been found helpful for reflecting on the ongoing nurturing relationship between a minister and a congregation, an abbot and those he is teaching and responsible for. The insights we can draw from some of the past usage can inform current ideas about ministry that may prove helpful for those engaged in Christian leadership.

Maternal imagery for Christian ministry has not, in the past, been linked to questions about the gender of the minister. Instead it has been about finding a metaphor for kind, caring, and involved nurturing. As Gaventa says of Paul's use of maternal metaphors, they describe the ongoing relationship, rather than the initiating ministry. Walker Bynum notes that for the Cistercians they spoke of ambivalence towards the power of leadership and arose out of a desire to express a more interdependent style of community.

Where the Church is described as mother it reminds Christians of their dependence on her for ongoing sustenance, and creates an image of a comforting, holding love in which her members are, in some sense, repeatedly born anew. Clearly, this imagery draws on fairly traditional ideas about mothering, especially where kindness and compassion are attributed to mothers and discipline to fathers. Yet, notwithstanding the traditional imagery, maternal images of the Church remind us that an important aspect of the ordained is to continually care for and nurture those entrusted to them and this involves a self-giving ministry. The image of breastfeeding is important here, for this self-giving, like breastfeeding, may be tiring at times but is not about diminishment. What is needed flows from mother to child and is replenished so long as the child needs feeding and the mother maintains her health. As I noted in the previous chapter, this breastfeeding imagery has something to say to us about grace, about being with and for the other and trusting that they will receive through that ministry what they need in order to flourish.

PART II
Mothering:
Gender, Theory and Practice

Chapter 4
Mothering: Gender and Culture

In the last chapter I explored examples of maternal imagery being used as an analogy for Christian ministry. As, historically, ministry has been a male preserve, these examples showed men drawing on female imagery to reflect on their own role. In the Church of England the roles of deacon and priest are now open to women, and the debate about women bishops is ongoing. The opening up of ordained ministry to women has been, and continues to be, contentious. Gendered metaphors for the role of the ordained are therefore contentious. Those who assert the importance of retaining an all-male priesthood are wary of any feminine language about ministry, and women in ministry feel ambiguous about gendered images and particularly the language of motherhood. In this chapter I will explore theories of gender that underpin the contention and ambiguity of using feminine imagery and, particularly, the language of mothering. The issue of how to discuss difference is paramount. Are gender differences an essential part of the natural order and, if so, to what extent do these differences dictate the roles appropriate to men and women? Or are gender differences a product of social construction? And where does the experience of motherhood and mothering fit into these debates? These are complex questions and there is a wealth of literature exploring gender and how it can be understood. Within the limits of this book I will not be able to do justice to all aspects of the debate, but I will endeavour to outline the main issues that impact on how motherhood and mothering are understood.

Essentialism – A Male-Only Priesthood

In the debates around the ordination of women, both to the priesthood and now as bishops, it is clear that many of the opponents have an essentialist understanding of gender difference. To defend a male-only priesthood is to assume that there is a difference between men and women that makes one suitable and the other unsuitable for the role of a priest or bishop. Essentialist theories of gender are then often combined with theories of ordination that are strongly Christological or rooted in a fixed interpretation of New Testament patterns of ministry. Thus it is argued that Jesus Christ was male and so his representatives need to be male. The twelve Apostles were male, therefore Jesus only authorised men and this needs to be continued. New Testament household codes point to man's headship of women, therefore men must be in authority over women.[1]

---

[1] The listed twelve Apostles are all male: Mark 3:16–19. Household codes in the New Testament suggest women's submission to their husbands: Colossians 3:18; 1 Corinthians 11:3–16.

All the above assertions depend on a clear difference between men and women, a difference that is not altered by women's education or liberation. Theologically this difference is located in Creation.[2] Men and women are affirmed as being made in the image of God, which confers a level of equality in humanity, but it is an equality that is manifest in sexual difference. This difference is seen in the centrality of reproduction: men beget children, and women conceive, birth and feed them. It is argued that these reproductive differences are signs of deeper differences. Essentialists can therefore affirm the equal worth of men and women while asserting that they are to be understood as complementary, each offering a difference that together makes the whole of humanity.

The late Pope, John Paul II, offers an example of an essentialist understanding of gender derived from God's creation of humanity as male and female. In a letter seeking to affirm the worth of women he wrote:

> Womanhood and manhood are complementary *not only from the physical and psychological points of view,* but also from the *ontological.* It is only through the duality of the 'masculine' and the 'feminine' that the 'human' finds full realisation.[3]

This ontological difference, a term that I noted was also used of the ordained priesthood, is a difference in the very being and nature of men and women. Defining men and women as ontologically different implies that they are different in ways that cannot be changed. Humanity, according to John Paul II's understanding, is fully realised in the duality or complementarity of the masculine and feminine. From the same letter he writes:

> In the Church's outlook, women and men have been called by the Creator to live in profound communion with one another, with reciprocal knowledge and giving of self, acting together for the common good with the complementary characteristics of that which is feminine and masculine.[4]

The assumption is that such complementary characteristics are clearly understood but, as we saw when discussing difference in terms of ministry, it is easier to assert difference than to define it. Outlining the differences becomes difficult, especially when education and broader cultural experiences seem to undermine historical assumptions. There are also interesting questions about who decides what the differences are.

---

[2]   The two Creation accounts in Genesis 1 and 2 both note the creation of humans as male and female. Genesis 1:27 simply states 'male and female he created them', while Genesis 2:18–23 describes the creation of woman out of Adam's rib.

[3]   Letter of Pope John Paul II, *To Women,* from the Vatican, 29 June 1995. www. vatican.va/holy_father/john_paulii/letters (12 March 2011).

[4]   Ibid.

For those who oppose women's inclusion in the ordained ministry, the essential differences between men and women reflect, at some level, truths about God and how God orders the world. Christ's masculinity is therefore an essential aspect of the incarnation. As we saw in the first chapter, such a theology of ordination is strongly Christological, so if Christ's masculinity is significant, priests need this same essential masculinity in order to represent Christ. Quoting John Paul II again, we find that in his understanding representation requires resemblance:

> The same natural resemblance is required for persons as for things: when Christ's role in the Eucharist is to be expressed sacramentally, there would not be this 'natural resemblance' which must exist between Christ and his minister if the role of Christ were not taken by a man: in such a case it would be difficult to see in the minister the image of Christ. For Christ himself was and remains a man.[5]

This is elaborated in modern Catholic theology by nuptial imagery, particularly through the writing of Hans Urs von Balthasar. Christ is the bridegroom who through his male priests 'comes to the Church, to make her fruitful'.[6] This theology can become quite complex in its imagery, as men and women are both feminine in the laity of the congregation, receiving the ministry from masculine priests, who must be men. To challenge the masculinity of these priests or to use feminine language about their role would be to undermine the distinctively masculine activity that is claimed to be essential to priesthood. Though what this distinctiveness is, is not clearly articulated.

A traditionally Protestant opposition to women's ordination is focused less on sacramental representation, revolving instead around ideas of male headship. An example of this can be found in an article by Carrie Sandham, a permanent deacon in the Church of England. She affirms God's ordering of male and female difference as biblical, pointing to creation and New Testament codes:

> Adam was created first as leader/provider (he gave the animals their names), and Eve was created second as the only suitable helper for him (she accepted both her generic name from him, as well as her specific name – see Genesis 2:23 and 3:20). Neither one was superior to the other, both were made in God's image and both were necessary to fulfil the creation mandate to fill the earth and subdue it (Genesis 1).

---

[5]   *Inter Insigniores*, 15 October 1976, Sacred Congregation for the Doctrine of Faith, www.papalencyclicals.net paragraph 5 (27 November 2012).

[6]   Quoted in Tina Beattie, *New Catholic Feminism* (Abingdon 2006), p. 133. Beattie outlines the complexity of this nuptial imagery and particularly the way in which men can represent both the masculine priesthood and the feminine Church, but women can only be receptive. 'A female body cannot be priest because the priest is male, but a male body can be bride because the bride is feminine but not necessarily female', p. 139.

This establishes the Biblical principle of male headship which is to be modelled in the Church (see 1 Corinthians 11 & 14, Titus 2 and 1 Timothy 2). Men are to take the position of overall leadership and will demonstrate their authority through teaching the whole congregation, while women are to help them in that role and, specifically, are needed to teach and train the women.[7]

Conservative groups such as Reform, on whose webpage Sandham's article was posted, espouse this view of women's different role and speak of a 'complementarian' view of ministry. They maintain that it is not about the subordination of women, though the passage above does seem to imply that, but the right understanding of male and female characteristics as God has intended. Men and women are, it is argued, equally valid in God's sight but in Creation God determines different ways of being and therefore different roles and areas of ministry.

The language of complementarity is used here by both Catholic and Protestant theologians to assert that differences in gender determine differences in ministerial role. This is a key aspect of essentialist views of gender; claims are universal and deterministic. However, they are not always used to argue for the subordination of women. An essentialist view of difference and complementarity can also be used to argue for women's inclusion in ministry. If women are different and humanity is only fully realised in both, then it can be argued that specifically female gifts are needed in ministry to reflect a fully rounded humanity. Such a feminist position idealises the accepted view of women's difference, particularly seeing women as nurturing and caring, and argues that these should be prioritised. Women are needed in the workplace and the Church to bring feminine values that will critique traditionally male ways of working. Thus we find one aspect of the writing in favour of women's ordination is the need for feminine ways of being to play their part in shaping and changing the Church.

Although complementarity it is argued affirms both men and women we find that women are not perceived as being able to cross gender divides, but the same is not true of men. Thus Sandham's conservative view of women's ministry argues that women's natural calling is to teach women and children. However, she then goes on to say that men can also do this, and she particularly stresses the need for men to be involved in the teaching of children. Men can and should teach women, but women should not teach men. In the Catholic nuptial imagery for the Church both men and women can be the feminine church receiving ministry but only men can represent Christ. Complementarity, therefore, seems to imply that women can complement men, rather than the other way round. Women are, at some level, an addendum to the masculine norm and only men can gender bend.

---

[7]   Carrie Sandham, 'The Biblical Pattern for Women's Ministry', published on the Reform website www.reform.org.uk. Reform is an Anglican evangelical organisation founded in 1993, just after the Church of England vote to allow the ordination of women as priests (15 November 2011).

Essentialist and Constructivist Theories of Gender

Clearly, it is not just in theological discussions that assumptions are made about feminine and masculine characteristics. Popular culture provides many books, articles and media discussions about the differences between men and women, often affirming traditional ideas about male assertiveness and rationality as opposed to female nurturance and increased ability to relate.[8] The majority of people would affirm that there are biological differences between men and women relating to hormones, sexual maturation, sexual organs and the roles played in reproduction.[9] The question is whether and how these differences determine broader characteristics and whether these differences should define the kinds of roles that women and men should fill.

Historical shifts in attitudes to women have challenged and changed the assumptions made about what women are naturally capable of doing. The movement of women's liberation has opened up education and many different spheres of work to women in many parts of the world, and challenged stereotypes that define all women as less rational or more nurturing. The movement towards equality between the sexes has raised important questions about what is assumed to be masculine and feminine, leading to a more fluid and less traditional understanding of characteristics and roles. Yet the lived experience of men and women continue to point to differences that seem to be present from childhood. Even when it is acknowledged that claims about male and female behaviour are not universal, they are often shown, at some level, to be general. Popular writing and academic studies seem to show that even if men and women are not universally different, there is enough generality to claim that there are women's and men's ways of doing things.

This has been important in trying to articulate ways in which women are subtly disadvantaged. Carol Gilligan's research published as *In a Different Voice: Psychological Theory and Women's Development* appears to show a general difference in the way women make moral decisions. In it she concludes that young men are more likely to use abstract ways of making decisions while young women explore the contextual and concrete issues, looking for a relationally satisfying answer. She claims that because traditional ways of assessing the maturity of moral decisions favours the abstract, girls have been defined as less mature.[10] Another influential study, *Women's Ways of Knowing: The Development of Self, Voice, and Mind*,[11] explores the experience of women in higher education. This study

---

[8]   A popular example is John Gray, *Men Are from Mars, Women Are from Venus* (London 1992), which sets out to explain relationships in terms of male and female difference.

[9]   It is important to acknowledge that some individuals are born with indeterminate sex.

[10]   Carol Gilligan, *In a Different Voice: Psychological Theory and Women's Development* (Cambridge 1982). In this book she critiques Kohlberg's *Stages of Moral Development*, which assumes the more abstract reasoning showed a greater moral maturity.

[11]   M.F. Belenky, B.M. Clinchy, N.R. Goldberger and J.M. Tarule, *Women's Ways of Knowing* (New York 1986).

concludes that women do less well under the adversarial style of teaching present in American universities and prosper under a more discursive pattern of learning. These studies resonated with many women's personal experience in the 1980s and continue to influence thinking today. Though some have criticised the size of the studies and the homogeneity of the subjects in terms of culture and race, they seem to confirm differences in the way women and men encounter the world.[12] Yet they do not necessarily suggest that these differences are essential or natural.

In asserting general differences in women's ways of thinking and acting, some feminists have argued that these are not the outer expression of biological differences or natural characteristics but are, instead, results of social and cultural conditioning. The theory of socially constructed gender argues that behaviour, patterns of thinking and acting, and even perhaps brain development, are shaped by the reinforced assumptions of socially accepted gender stereotypes. According to this theory, girls and boys, women and men learn to behave in ways that accord to cultural assumptions about their gender.

Iris Marion Young's article 'Throwing Like a Girl'[13] provides an interesting comment on how early these gender assumptions begin to cement patterns of behaviour. She explores how girls and boys learn to use their bodies differently pre-puberty when, in fact, there are few bodily differences. Boys learn to throw with their whole bodies while girls, who have been taught to contain their bodies, simply throw with their arms. Through the role models offered and the affirmations given, boys learn to be masculine and girls feminine according to the cultural norms. Differences, she concludes, are not inherent, shaped by biology, but are learned through the subtle processes of reinforcement in which boys and girls generally conform to expected gender behaviour. Young's reflection on the bodily ways children learn to behave is a useful reminder about how human beings learn and develop through imitating those they aspire to be like.

The anthropologist Marcel Mauss[14] describes how children and adults imitate those they trust and in the end develop movements such as walking that seem 'natural'. It may then be assumed that they are instinctual; however, such natural movements might well have been subtly different if learned from someone else in a different cultural setting. He calls this 'prestigious imitation' and notes that it stretches from practices that an individual had knowingly copied to ways

---

[12]   The Womanist movement, which grew out of responses to the novel *The Colour Purple* by Alice Walker, published in 1982, is one of the movements to critique these studies. Womanist theory arises out of the experience of black women and argues for a proper understanding of the role that race and class plays in oppression, so white women's experience cannot be seen as definitive of black or other marginalised groups. Gilligan and Belenky's work is seen as primarily white, educated and middle class.

[13]   Iris Marion Young, 'Throwing Like a Girl', in Donn Welton (ed.), *Body and Flesh* (Oxford 1998), pp. 259–73.

[14]   Marcel Mauss, *The Notion of Body Techniques in Sociology and Psychology*, translated by Ben Brewster (London 1979).

of behaving that had been learned without conscious reflection. He was not writing about gender differences, but cultural ones; however, knowing that even seemingly natural bodily movements are learned is helpful in thinking about how gender differences are inhabited. So if girls and boys are encouraged through social expectations to imitate older members of their own gender, they will begin to behave bodily in ways that correlate to what is recognisably masculine and feminine within their culture. Because this happens at a level that is not articulated or necessarily reflected on, it can appear to be natural, and through habitual behaviour the body itself adapts to what it has learned.

If we follow Young's examples of throwing balls we can find that a girl brought up in a family full of boys may well be labelled as a 'tomboy' because she inhabits her body in a more recognisably masculine way and throws like her brothers. She may be indulged in this, but cultural norms might also suggest that at some point she needs to re-educate herself into more feminine behaviour. Thus gendered behaviour, even where it can appear natural, can be understood as being socially constructed. As cultural acceptance of different ways of being masculine and feminine develop, so differences may be more easily tolerated.

However, to accept that gender behaviour is socially constructed does not remove the many issues that exist because of sexual differences. What it does mean is that once gender differences are not seen as fixed by nature, they can be challenged and diversity can be encouraged. A socially constructed understanding of gender differences can also allow gender to be seen as part of a variety of differences, like race, culture, class or wealth, and may not be the most important or pressing factor in addressing particular issues.[15] A socially constructed view of gender critiques ideas about universal gender behaviour, acknowledging that different cultures can affirm very different patterns of 'the feminine'. It also follows that because gender characteristics are shaped by culture, the language of complementarity is misleading; instead the equality of human beings is stressed and role stereotypes are challenged. Theologically this position finds its basis in the common humanity created in the *imago Dei*. What matters is that we are all created as human. Specific characteristics and ways of behaving are not allocated to each sex but are human, and therefore men and women can learn from each other and develop similar human capacities.

There is both historical and cultural evidence to support many of the assertions of socially constructed gender theory. Through opening up education and the workplace to women it is clear that women are able to do and to think in ways that were previously assumed to be unfeminine. Different cultures offer different assumptions about the feminine and masculine so that in some parts of the world women are deemed weak, unable to engage in heavy manual work, while in other

---

[15]   Womanist theology, for instance, will say that there are many issues where the colour of someone's skin is a more significant difference than their gender. Where racial oppression is prevalent, black men and women have more in common than a white woman and a black woman in terms of the ways they have been categorised and oppressed.

places they are expected to carry heavy loads. Understanding different cultural assumptions about gender can challenge stereotypes and open up new possibilities for women and men. Yet gender difference, however it is construed, is still significant across cultures. Babies are recognised, with rare exceptions, as male or female at birth[16] and the later experiences of puberty and, for many, childbearing further define the differences. The assumptions about gender mean that men and women are often shaped by different experiences that then feed into the ways in which they think and act.

It therefore follows that a socially constructed theory of gender still has to contend with the lived experience of sexual difference. In defining the origins of this difference in culture rather than nature, a socially constructed view challenges both the universalism and determinism of essentialist theories. This is important, as it makes it possible to challenge the ways in which gender stereotypes have led and still can lead to the oppression of women and minorities that do not conform to culturally accepted norms. However, when difference is minimised or dismissed, in order to affirm the equality of men and women, areas of experience that have been predominantly female can be marginalised or silenced. This is of particular interest for the subject of mothering which is clearly connected to both physical sexual difference and cultural assumptions. Is there a way of highlighting such embodied differences of women that does not lead to a complementarity that marginalises or idealises women's lived experience?

The Problem of Difference – Irigaray and Questions of Subjectivity

It is this question of whether we can find a middle path through essentialist and constructivist ways of understanding difference that interests the French feminist philosopher Luce Irigaray. Her contention is that when common humanity and working for equality becomes the primary focus, then the actuality of women's experiences, especially bodily experiences, and the differences that are part of many women's lives may, in fact, be ignored – to the detriment of women. She poses the question: what does equality mean?

> Demanding equality, as women, seems to me to be an erroneous expression of a real issue. Demanding to be equal presupposes a term of comparison. Equal to what? What do women want to be equal to? Men? A wage? A public position? Equal to what? Why not themselves ... Egalitarianism, in fact, sometimes expends a lot of energy on rejecting certain positive values and chasing after nothing.[17]

---

[16]   Like most new mothers, the first thing I was told about my new born baby was his sex and that determined the name I gave him.

[17]   Luce Irigaray, 'Equal or Different', in Margaret Whitford (ed.), *The Irigaray Reader* (Oxford 1991), p. 32.

Thus even though the language of equality is at one level challenging the language of complementarity, it may unwittingly continue to compound the undervaluing of predominantly female ways of thinking and acting.

Irigaray maintains that this is a linguistic problem. We do not have a language that can talk meaningfully about difference. Thus the question is less about trying to understand the origins of gender difference and more about finding a language of inter-subjectivity: of two subjects. This is difficult because difference is most often articulated through binaries, where one thing is differentiated from the other by making one the subject and the other the object. In the earlier chapter on ministry I noted how difficult it was to articulate the difference between the ordained and the laity without resorting to such binaries. In that example, as in the example of gender, there is a tendency to privilege one over the other, using one as the norm from which the other differs. Thus men become the norm from which women are different.

Irigaray is not alone in asserting this as a problem. Many writers have noted the way that gender differences are associated with other binaries and the way that these privilege the masculine. Male/female connects to soul/body, rationality/emotion, and culture/nature. This has been particularly noted by feminist theologians because women have generally been associated with the body and matter, while the divine is imaged as masculine. Irigaray claims that the experiences of women's lives are under-articulated and thus undervalued, because woman is the object, never the subject. Margaret Whitford comments on Irigaray's writings:

> She warns against displacing the male/female binary before the female side has acceded to identity and subjectivity. To omit the question of the woman-as-subject and her identity in thought and culture is to leave in place a tenacious and damaging imaginary structure.[18]

It is for this reason that Irigaray focuses on the physical differences between men and women as a starting point for reflecting on sexual difference. She asserts that bodily differences matter. She reflects on the very different nature of male and female genitalia and sexual pleasure, asserting that women's bodies point to a plurality and openness; what she calls 'this sex which is not one'.[19] She critiques Freud's understanding of female development and sexuality and its assertion that 'penis envy' offers a satisfactory account of female development. She also reflects both on the importance of mothers and the ways in which they have been silenced and subjugated. She concludes that mothers have been reduced to 'a mere

---

[18]   Ibid., p. 13.

[19]   Luce Irigaray, *Ce sexe qui n'en est pas un* (Paris 1977); Luce Irigaray, translated by Catherine Porter, *This Sex Which Is Not One* (Ithaca 1985).

function',[20] and elsewhere says that they have been 'defined as a thing'.[21] Women, she argues, need to find their subjectivity and mothers need to find ways of not losing their sense of their own selves as women in the role of mothering. I will return to the importance of this in the following chapter when discussing child development. That chapter will look at other critiques of Freud and argue for an inter-subjective understanding of the mother/child relationship.

Critics accuse Irigaray of essentialism because she affirms that there *are* sexual differences and that women's bodily differences are significant. However, she is not claiming a universalistic or deterministic view of difference. Instead she is critiquing the way the language of equality, while challenging important issues of female oppression, has unwittingly colluded in undervaluing women. Attempts to de-gender language still perpetuate oppositional binaries that privilege traditionally masculine attributes. Irigaray writes in French, so is using a language that is more obviously gendered, and she notes that when a crowd is mixed, even if the majority of people are women, in French it takes the masculine form. Thus, she argues, gender-neutral terminology tends to perpetuate the idea that things are more valid when men participate. This is one of my reasons for consciously using a gendered term in this book. A gender-neutral term like parenting changes, at some level, the way care of children is viewed, because it no longer defines the work with a feminine word.

In retaining a feminine term for describing the practice of caring for children I am not suggesting that men should not or cannot participate. There has been a welcome cultural shift in expectations about men's engagement with children. However, a gender-neutral term fails to acknowledge both the reality that child-rearing is still principally undertaken by women and still undervalued because it is women's work. Men who have taken on the primary care of their own children recognise this undervaluing. Yet we find it difficult to accept that a feminine word could be used to positively describe work undertaken by men as well as women.

As the book unfolds it will become clear that the practice of mothering is made up of ways of thinking and acting that are not gender-specific, though they may be more commonly practised by women. However, it must be acknowledged that the specifically female bodily experience of pregnancy, childbirth and lactation all impact on women's readiness to mother and can shape some of these ways of thinking and acting. It follows that to talk about mothering and to find ways of articulating and privileging some of the ways of thinking and acting that arise from the practice, it is necessary to understand and acknowledge that this is an area where sexual difference exists. Women's bodily experience in childbearing is an essential sexual difference. In fact, one of the main complexities of mothering is that it does not fit into a neat binary. The bodily experiences of having a child do not have an

---

[20]   Luce Irigaray, 'Women – Mothers: the Silent Substratum', pp. 47–52, in Whitford, *The Irigaray Reader*, p. 50.

[21]   Luce Irigaray, 'Sexual Difference', pp. 165–77, in Whitford, *The Irigaray Reader*, p. 169.

equivalent in male experience. It is perhaps for this reason that motherhood has been mythologised and idealised. Yet this idealisation diminishes the actuality of the practice. It has tended to subjugate and silence mothers' experience and has not led to a proper valuing of the learning, work and skills involved. In acknowledging the sexual differences inherent in the birthing of children I still want to resist the language of complementarity, because to acknowledge that aspects of human life arise out of the reality of sexual difference is not to assume that the things learned through such experiences belong to either gender. In particular, it does not follow that women are in any way more naturally caring.

One of the ways of challenging the determinism of gender essentialism is to locate difference in characteristics, ways of thinking and acting, rather than a specific sex. Thus characteristics are designated as masculine or feminine even though they can be appropriated by men and women. For example a man who is caring and empathetic may be described as 'in touch with his feminine side'. Despite the seeming freedom for characteristics to be utilised by both genders, the assumption that they are gendered in themselves perpetuates binaries and unhelpfully categorises ideas like empathy as feminine and rationality as masculine, whether possessed by a man or a woman. Imaging these differences as opposites means people are assumed to be either more rational or more intuitive, rather than being able to be intuitively rational. Gendering such attributes means the stereotypes of masculine ordered rationality opposed to feminine empathy and intuition are maintained with all the history of privileging objective rationality over feelings.

Irigaray challenges the assumption that there has to be an either/or. She argues that we need to properly explore and value the areas designated feminine. For, unless what is designated as feminine is valued, women are urged to find equality by adapting to masculine capacities without the resources to critique them. As Rosemary Radford Ruether concludes:

> Women, through the opening of equal education and political rights, have indeed demonstrated their ability to exercise the 'same' capacities as men ... Liberalism assumes the traditional male sphere as normative and believes it is wrong to deny people access to it on the basis of gender. But once women are allowed to enter the public sphere, liberalism offers no critique of the modes of functioning within it.[22]

By challenging stereotypical ideas about what is masculine and feminine it is possible to challenge the notion of opposition; to think rationally does not need to equate to thinking abstractly and disinterestedly. To make space for feelings and emotions is not to lose sight of reason, but may involve reasoning differently.

When we consider the practice of mothering we find a complex mix of biological bodily difference and culturally conditioned learning. This has meant

---

[22]   Rosemary Ruether, *Sexism and God-Talk* (London 1983), p. 110.

that many women have developed ways of thinking and acting that are different from men, whose bodily and cultural experiences have been very different. The constructivist view of sexual difference reminds us how much that appears to be natural is in fact learned. Thus women, who have been engaged in caring for children, have had to cope with very different ideas about change and fluidity from men or *women* who have not shared these experiences but have instead been involved in manufacturing products or abstract thinking. So it is possible to talk about ways of thinking and acting that have been predominantly female because more women have had to develop such ways of thinking and acting in order to manage the experiences and responsibilities of their lives. The difficulty is in finding the language to articulate such experiences without them being marginalised and relegated to 'women's stuff'. In finding an appropriate language, the idea that there is a normative experience of humanity needs to be challenged and the value of diversity of experience taken seriously.

To summarise the discussion so far, we note that although the significance of sexual difference is present across cultures, defining such differences, beyond basic biology, is problematic. The historical dominance of men means that such definitions tend to privilege the masculine norm over the feminine other. Changes in education and society have clearly highlighted that universal and deterministic claims about male and female roles linked to their gendered capacities are unfounded. Yet differences persist. Cultural assumptions and the subtle ways that these are reinforced can explain many aspects of gender difference but despite the claims of some,[23] bodily differences also play a part. Through a complex mix of these factors many women have developed capacities for thinking and acting in ways that differ in certain circumstances from the predominantly male tradition. Irigaray makes an important point in arguing that such ways of thinking and acting are often under-articulated and defined as other or inferior to a masculine norm. It also follows that in rejecting simplistic concepts of male and female nature, the human capacity to learn how to think and act in different ways is affirmed. Thus ways of being and behaving that have been attributed to a particular gender can potentially be learned by both men and women: just as women can learn from male experience, so men can learn from the insights and experiences of women.

At the beginning of this chapter I noted that in using maternal imagery and language for ministry I am challenging assumptions about the essentially male nature of the priestly role, but I am not seeking to claim a privilege for women in ministry. The preceding argument has made it clear that drawing on a female image does not directly correlate to the gender of the priest. We saw in the previous chapter that on occasions men were comfortable in drawing analogies between their ministry and maternal experiences. I would argue that the inclusion of women,

---

[23]   Judith Butler, in *Gender Trouble: Feminism and the Subversion of Identity* (London 1990), introduces the concept of gender performity, which claims that gender is never fixed and even the physiological differences traditionally accepted as fixed points of difference can be challenged as constructions of gender.

or the possible inclusion of women, in the role of priest has made many men and women more resistant to such metaphors because it is assumed to be a privileging of the female. As Ruether argued, and Irigaray implies, access to traditionally male spheres for women has usually involved encouraging a gender-neutral stance that downplays specifically female experiences. Clare Walsh's paper, which looks at the way women describe themselves before and after the inclusion of women in the priesthood in the Church of England, notes the desire to de-gender their role once they are in the male sphere of ordained ministry.

> Some women priests have chosen to distance themselves from the identity criteria of sex, sexuality and gender that were necessarily to the fore in the pre-ordination campaign. Instead, they emphasise the institutional force of their ordination as priests and insist that gender is largely irrelevant to the exercise of many aspects of their sacerdotal role … The implication is that the gender-marking of what should be a gender-neutral occupational role is an unnecessary distraction.[24]

She quotes one of the women she has interviewed: 'whether you're a woman or a man shouldn't make any difference at all – I feel your gender should disappear in a service' and goes on to comment about 'her rejection of the "feely" and "personal" aspects of some women's approach to ministry, and of their propensity to "go on endlessly about birth"'.[25] Walsh comments that this de-gendering of the role is particularly interesting, as the role of priest seems to embody characteristics that have been traditionally designated feminine. She notes the reluctance of the women she interviewed to use any feminine analogies:

> This is particularly paradoxical, since priestly ministry is, in many ways, a feminine occupation. Indeed, priesthood can be seen as an instance of socially and institutionally sanctioned gender-crossing behaviour by men.[26]

Fears expressed by male priests that the increase in women clergy is 'feminising' the Church points to a continuing sense that areas that are labelled as feminine tend to be seen as less valuable and for women only. Yet, I would argue, by failing to acknowledge the ways in which parish ministry utilises what have been traditionally understood as feminine characteristics, we are in danger of privileging aspects of ministry that relate to more traditionally masculine ways of working at the expense of much that has been and is valuable in the day-to-day ministry of parish priests as it has been done by men and now, also, by women.

---

[24] Clare Walsh, *Speaking in Different Tongues*, a Sheffield Hallam Working Paper on the Web, www.shu.ac.uk (12 March 2011). She is quoting one of the ordained women she interviewed.

[25] Ibid.

[26] Ibid.

Chapter 5
Mothering: Questions of Instinct and Inter-Subjectivity

In this book I am taking a female image and deliberately using feminine language to explore the role of priest as undertaken by men and women. It would have been possible to choose the gender-neutral term 'parenting' to explore child-rearing. However, for the majority of people, the care they received as young children was predominantly carried out by a woman or women. Patterns of child-rearing are changing and many fathers participate in caring, but it is important to acknowledge the cultural assumptions that still designate childcare as women's work. In time this position may well seem dated, but at present the reality is that childcare is mainly undertaken by women, and the men who engage in full-time childcare are seen as unusual. Therefore many of the skills learned and ways of thinking developed have been designated as female, with associated implications for the ways they are valued. I also want to acknowledge that the majority of mothers have had the bodily experience of pregnancy and childbirth; many will also have breastfed their children. As I will argue later, I do not think that these experiences are a necessity for good mothering, but they are a factor that impacts on those who have experienced them. While acknowledging that the elision of women and the maternal has been a problematic stereotype, it is important to resist the silencing of maternal experience and the lack of recognition of all that the practice and imagery can offer.

The physical process of bearing children is a uniquely female experience, an example of specificity and difference. Although women's bodies are, on the whole, configured so that they can have children, not all women want to have children and some women want them but find that they are unable to have them. Yet, all children are born to a woman. Cultural differences will play their part in how pregnancy, childbirth and breastfeeding are experienced and narrated, but they will always be experiences that are specific to female bodies. It is because children are born to women, alongside women's ability to lactate in order to feed them, that it has been assumed that women have a special ability to nurture and care for children. This physical reality has been underpinned by the presumption of a maternal instinct, which implies that there is a *natural* response from a mother to care for her child. An essentialist view of gender might well go further and say that it is this maternal instinct that enables women to care for more than just her biological children; women are naturally nurturing. Yet, the term instinct, I would argue, undervalues mothering because it implies an unthinking response and a reactive behaviour. Therefore, I will suggest that mothering should not be understood as an instinctual reaction but as an active commitment to a relationship.

The gender-neutral term 'parenting' is emotively different from the language of mothering and it is not usually understood as instinctual. Through books and courses it is implied that parenting skills can be learned; you can attend parenting classes and courses or read books on improving parenting skills. In a helpful article Caroline Whitbeck comments thus:

> When people talk about maternal instincts, what they seem to be discussing are the inner promptings, which induce women to care for their offspring. All this is frequently supposed to be connected with love in some way, and may even be considered a particular species of love. What complicates the matter is that whereas we do speak of parental affection, and paternal as well as maternal feelings, there is no talk of *paternal instincts* ... It would seem, therefore, that while certain feelings may be viewed as characteristic of parents of both sexes, in women this parental affectation is viewed as augmented or enhanced in some special way.[1]

It is this idea of an augmented or enhanced maternal love that is popularly understood to make women, naturally, more able and willing to nurture and care for young children. This instinct is offered as an explanation for women's desire to have children and her inbuilt capacity to nurture them. However, female experience does not always correlate to assumptions about an instinctual ability to love and care for one's child. The anxiety, ambivalence and difficulties that some mothers have with all aspects of mothering and many have with some aspects, points to a more complex process of learning how to care for infants.[2] This ambivalence has been well documented in feminist writings on motherhood many of which have sought to challenge accepted ideas of maternal love.[3] Thus although it is certainly true that the majority of caring for babies and young children is carried out by women, frequently the biological mother of the child, it does not necessarily follow that this is because women are simply allowing a natural instinct to kick in, or that they are uniquely capable of providing such care.

---

[1]   Caroline Whitbeck, 'The Maternal Instinct', in Joyce Trebilcot, *Mothering* (Totowa 1984), p. 186.

[2]   This is true even of the physiological aspect of breastfeeding. It is clear that many women find a process that is at one level natural extremely difficult to establish. Women may well need help and advice to *learn* how to breastfeed.

[3]   Adrienne Rich, *Of Woman Born* (New York 1976) looked at the way the institution of motherhood, which she saw as a product of patriarchy, oppressed women and limited their capacity to experience positive aspects of mothering. In her book she speaks of the ambivalence she felt at times towards her children, 'the murderous alternation between bitter resentment and raw-edged nerves and blissful gratification'. The subject of maternal ambivalence continues to be a cause for challenging idealised views of mothering. Rachel Cusk's 2001 *A Life's Work* explored in detail her complex, ambiguous feelings towards the experience of motherhood.

Why Do Women Mother: Is There a Maternal Instinct?

Socially constructed theories of gender have sought to understand mothering by seeking to minimise the bodily experience and focus on social, political and psychoanalytical ideas. They have thus dismissed ideas of a natural maternal instinct. Nancy Chodorow in *The Reproduction of Mothering* argues that a maternal instinct is a social construct. It is worth noting her use of the term parenting rather than mothering:

> When we evaluate claims for the instinctual or biological basis for parenting, it turns out that evidence is hard to find.[4]

She uses psychoanalytical theory to argue that because it's predominantly women who care for children, both men and women are conditioned into stereotypical gender roles in parenthood. Her work has been influential in arguing that women take on the role of mothering because women have mothered them rather than in response to a maternal instinct. This, she claims, has an impact beyond mothering, from how boys and girls are socialised to ideas about caring.

Following Freud she discusses the way that boys individuate from their mother by becoming different, while girls seek, in the end, to be like their mothers. Because, in Chodorow's understanding, mothers see girls as like them, girls learn to identify with their own mothers and to internalise the importance of the nurturing role, especially in terms of childcare. Boys, on the other hand, develop their sense of self by differentiating from their mothers, and in doing so, need to distance themselves from the maternal tasks. This, she maintains, is internalised, with boys learning to see practical nurturing care as women's work.

Chodorow uses a basically Freudian theory of child development. Freud's theory of developmental stages has been particularly important as a way of explaining sexual difference. He maintained that infants pass through different stages of fixation, driven by subliminal sexual desires, beginning with an oral stage, focusing on the pleasure of being nursed, moving on to an anal stage, connected to potty training, and then the phallic or oedipal stage. It is this last stage in which Freud argued that boys and girls learn to differentiate their sexual identities. Boys, he argued, are frustrated by their mother's desire for their father and feel, firstly, anger towards the father as a rival for her love and then, recognising the father's power, they desire to become like the father. In doing so they reject the mother, who has no penis and whom they fear might castrate them. Through this process boys identify themselves as masculine and individuate themselves from the world of the maternal.

Freud was less clear about female development, offering an oedipal theory sometimes referred to as the Electra complex. Girls at this stage, he argued,

---

[4]   Nancy Chodorow, *The Reproduction of Mothering* (Berkeley 1978; new edn 1999), p. 23.

become aware of their lack of a penis and that their mother also shares this lack. This leads to desire for the father, anger towards the mother, whom they hold responsible for this castration, and eventually a movement to be like the mother because that is whom the father desires. Freud maintained that girls never fully resolve this oedipal stage and that the desire for children replaces the ongoing sense of a lack of a penis.

Freud's theories have had an important impact on ideas about child development and, especially, the need for a child to separate from the world of the mother in order to find his own sense of identity and autonomy. For Chodorow this rejection of the world of the mother on the part of boys leads men to reject caring, nurturing roles, associating these with the maternal world. She differs from Freud in claiming that a girl's process through the oedipal stage does not require the repression of her earlier attachments, meaning that she develops a more complex ability to relate, care and nurture. Altering the care that children receive in these early years of development so that both men and women nurture the young, she claims, could allow a more complex relational attitude in boys as well as girls, changing, in time, the way men and women view caring and nurturing roles.

As I noted earlier, Irigaray criticises Freud because his developmental theory offers a very limited understanding of women and their sexuality.[5] She maintains that Freudian theories of individuation from the mother have denied the subjectivity of the mother and focused on a rejection of the maternal which she describes as a kind of 'matricide'. Jessica Benjamin, a feminist psychoanalyst, also challenges the assumption that separation or rejection of the mother is a necessary part of human individuation.[6] She, like Irigaray, argues for a sense of inter-subjectivity and an understanding of the mother/child relationship that is based on mutual recognition.

Although I do not follow Chodorow's Freudian explanation of sexual difference her work raises important points about how boys and girls are socialised into attitudes towards parenting roles and caring roles in general. Because the majority of people have a primary caretaker who is female, most often the biological mother, this leads both male and female children to assume mothering is female work and to extrapolate that caring in general is a feminine task. Many would concur with Chodorow's conclusion that a move to child-rearing that is equally shared between men and women could alter attitudes to both child-rearing and more general caring roles.

Clearly, role models, social expectations and culturally reinforced assumptions about women's capacity to mother all play an important part in the way that women

---

[5]   Luce Irigaray, 'The Power of Discourse and the Subordination of the Feminine', in Whitford, *The Irigaray Reader*, p. 119.

[6]   Jessica Benjamin, *The Bonds of Love: Psychoanalysis, Feminism and the Problem of Domination* (New York 1988). She stills sees issues around individuation and assertion of independence but these arise out of a relationship of mutual recognition and are about a failure in inter-subjectivity.

tend to assume the major responsibility of caring for their children. Yet, I do not think that it is possible to explain why women mother without reflecting on the bodily experiences connected to mothering. I would argue that specific physical differences between the sexes do play a part, not through a biological instinct, but through the particular way that women become mothers. As Caroline Whitbeck concludes:

> Parental affection or attachment is influenced by experience, and this experience is not confined to socialisation experience, but includes, in large measure, bodily experiences that are the same cross-culturally; i.e., all women have special bodily experiences that are likely to enhance those feelings, attitudes, and fantasies, which induce people generally to care for their infants.[7]

She comments that 'these experiences do not readily fall into either the nature category or the nurture category'.[8] Sarah Blaffer Hrdy would concur with this:

> Instead of old dichotomies about nature versus nurture, attention needs to be focused on the complicated interactions among genes, tissue, glands, past experiences and environmental cues, including sensory cues provided by infants themselves and by other individuals in the vicinity. Complex behaviour like nurturing, especially when tied to even more complex emotions like 'love', are never genetically predetermined or environmentally produced.[9]

In *Mother Nature* Hrdy uses a Darwinian understanding of natural selection to look at the role of mothers in various species, including human beings. As we see from the quote above, she concludes that mothering in humans cannot be explained simply as instinctual behaviour, yet the bodily experience matters. She explores the impact of this experience, including the hormones released in pregnancy, birth and lactation. All these, she argues, are meant to promote a sense of attachment to the baby and have an effect. However, these hormones cannot fully explain why women commit to the care of their children; their impact is not significant enough. She also shows that human mothers are most likely to abandon their baby immediately after birth or in the very early days when one would assume a hormonal, biological instinct would kick in. Unlike herding animals, the human mother and baby do not instantly bond, but instead develop attachment over time as the mother commits to the child and begins to build a relationship with him.

Hrdy argues that human mothers need to actively commit to their child in order to develop this relationship. The period of gestation and the physical investment a mother has already made by the time the child is born means that in a majority of circumstances the mother is already committed to the well-being of the child, so

---

[7] Whitbeck, *The Maternal Instinct*, p. 191.

[8] Ibid., p. 186.

[9] Sarah Blaffer Hrdy, *Mother Nature* (New York 1999), p. 174.

is likely to commit to caring for him. The process of having a baby is physically costly for women. It takes up substantial time and energy and towards the end of pregnancy limits what a woman can do. Hrdy claims that, as a consequence of this investment of time and energy, mothers have a primary desire to invest in the future of the infant they have produced, so long as the circumstances are right. This desire to invest time and energy in the reality of a life that has already taken up time and energy promotes a relational attachment that enables the mother to respond attentively to the infant's needs. The hormones help, as does the vulnerability of the infant, yet predominantly a woman's prior experience encourages her to continue to care for this child. For a woman who feels positive about a pregnancy, the sense of attachment can begin before the child's birth. The reality of this attachment is established in the early days and weeks of a child's life, where closeness to one caregiver will begin to develop recognition from the child, which in turn strengthens the emotional bond between the mother or caregiver and that particular infant. What begins as a projected relationship, or even as an anticipated relationship, becomes a real relationship in which the responses of the baby play an important part.

Infants need to be cared for and, Hrdy argues, human babies have evolved to appeal in ways that will strengthen the relationship with their primary caretakers. We will see when we look further at mothering how important the relationship and reciprocity between a baby and her primary caretakers is. Hrdy points out though that 'caretakers need not be the mother, or even one person, but they have to be the same caretakers'.[10] She concludes:

> Rather than some magical 'essence of mother,' what makes a mother maternal is that she is (invariably) at the scene, hormonally primed, sensitive to infant signals, and related to the baby. These factors lower her threshold for giving of herself to satisfy the infant's needs. Once her milk comes in, the mother's urge to nurture grows stronger still … These factors make the mother the likeliest candidate to become the primary caretaker. *But they do not constitute an unyielding prescription.*[11]

The reality is that if the mother does not take responsibility, others have to, or the baby will not survive. There is good evidence that women and men who are not the biological parent of a child can become the primary caregiver and invest in caring for and nurturing the infant.[12] It is also clear that mothering can be shared

---

[10]   Ibid., p. 508.

[11]   Ibid., p. 500.

[12]   Adoption of babies by relatives or through formal adoption programmes has long been part of human culture, especially where mothers die in childbirth, or have too many children. There has also been a long history of wealthy families entrusting the care of infants and children to paid nannies. What has been less satisfactory is where babies and infants are cared for in environments where they do not have consistent caretakers.

between a small number of individuals. Hrdy also notes that in circumstances where a woman feels unable or unwilling to care for the child she has borne, she may choose to abandon the child or, in extremis, kill it.[13]

Hrdy's description of the complex mix of biological and social factors that make it likely that a woman will take responsibility for the care of her infants offers a middle way between essentialist and constructivist views. Clearly, any position that speaks generally of the effects of hormones and bodily experiences specific to women is making some kind of universal claim about women and their sexual difference. These specifically female bodily experiences are significant factors in a woman choosing to take responsibility for nurturing her children. However, biology alone cannot explain why women care for their children; cultural and social factors will affect how a woman interprets her bodily experiences of pregnancy and birthing and her decision to mother her child. Thus non-biological factors also play a significant part in the assumption that the mother should become the primary carer. Due to the vulnerability of the infant, somebody has to care for it. The physical and emotional differences between a woman who is caught up in the experience of having a child, and a man or woman who is not, does make it more likely that the particular woman will take on the responsibility of caring. However, there is an element of choice: a choice that is circumscribed by social expectations and the particularities of the mother's situation. Where a mother chooses not to, or is unable to, become attached to the child, someone else will need to take on the responsibility.

It follows that whoever commits to the child and accepts the responsibility to care and nurture does not do so instinctually, but has to develop the relationship and learn how to care. Again, social expectations and modelling may well make it easier for women to learn these skills, but that does not mean they are *essentially* female skills. The ongoing work of caring for a baby, and later a child, develops because of the commitment to the relationship. Even those who have given birth to a child need to *learn* the myriad of skills needed to nurture its growth and development. Whereas the birthing experience draws on specifically female attributes, the ongoing work of care and nurture, aside from breastfeeding, cannot be connected to any female physiology. The experience of pregnancy may mean that mothers begin to think differently about bodies, time, and what can and cannot be controlled, which can help them adapt to the ways of thinking necessary for mothering, but often the experience of pregnancy leaves women feeling unprepared for the reality of the child. Whoever takes on the primary care of the infant enters a steep learning curve as they develop the necessary skills to enable the child to flourish. These skills must be learned through practice. This is true whether the biological mother or another caregiver takes up the responsibility.

---

[13] Abandonment or infanticide is a reality of most cultures, especially in times of poverty or where bearing a child in the wrong social situation would make it hard to acknowledge the child. In some cultures the gender of the child or her disability may lead to a decision to neglect or abandon her.

This responsibility of caring for a baby and growing child can be shared with others; children can attach to a small number of caring adults who together provide the loving, responsive care that they need. Yet, it makes sense to use the term mothering for this work as it has principally been undertaken by mothers. In using the terms mothering and mothers, I am including those men who are fathers but take on substantial responsibility for childcare and those men or women who through adoption, fostering or employment provide day-to-day care for children to whom they are not related by birth. I acknowledge that there may well be subtle differences in the way biological fathers or mothers relate to the children they care for, but I do not believe these differences are any more significant than the differences that might be found between those who wanted or did not want children, those of different social or educational status, or those who are financially secure and those who are not. Despite these myriad differences in the circumstances and expectations of those mothering, they are all engaged in a relationship that demands care. For Ruddick this demand for care is threefold. Her theory will be more fully explored in a later chapter. At this point I will simply quote her summary of the demands imposed on anyone doing maternal work:

> In this sense of demand, children 'demand' that their lives be preserved and their growth fostered. In addition, the primary social groups with which a mother is identified, whether by force, kinship, or choice, demand that she raise her children in a manner acceptable to them. These three demands – for *preservation, growth*, and *social acceptability* – constitute maternal work; to be a mother is to be committed to meeting these demands by works of preservative love, nurturance, and training.[14]

Attachment and Inter-Subjectivity

Central to the practice of mothering is the relationship between the mother and child. I noted above that Freudian theories have played an important part in ideas about child development. Freud focused on the internal and subliminal perceptions of the child: what the infant projected onto his mother, father and other caretakers. He understood the pre-oedipal relationship of the mother and infant to be one in which the identities were merged; that is, mother and child experienced themselves as one. As we will see, this concept of merged identity tends to suppress the subjectivity of the mother.

Freud's work was developed through working with adults reflecting back on their childhood experiences. Melanie Klein, having worked as a Freudian psychoanalyst in Germany, moved to London shortly before Freud's death. She analysed children as well as adults and claimed that the infant's sense of his own

---

[14]   Ibid., p. 17.

separate ego developed earlier than Freud's oedipal stage.[15] Klein argued that the young infant, at the nursing stage, was already involved in a complex mixture of love for the mother and fear of losing her, thus beginning to understand her separate reality. Klein maintained that by the oral stage the child perceived the mother, or her breast, as a separate object that could be both loved and hated.

Klein therefore pushes back the stage at which a child begins to perceive the mother as other. However, both Freud's and Klein's models of infant development focus entirely on the inner life of the child. They place great importance on the mother's ability to satisfy and frustrate the infant. Yet neither is interested in the mother as a subject. The infant, it is maintained, needs to move from a sense of being at one with the mother in some kind of merged reality, into a differentiation from the mother, which is usually characterised as a form of repudiation and rejection of the maternal. This sense of separation, it is argued, comes through processing the experience of being frustrated when desires are not met. The process of developing subjectivity is thus understood to arise out of perceived failures in response and a growing independence rather than a developing understanding of appropriate response and interdependence.

John Bowlby was a student of Klein's but moved away from the standard psychoanalytical position through his own observation of how children miss their parents. He came to profoundly disagree with the psychoanalytical fixation on a child's inner life.[16] The mother was not, he argued, simply an object to satisfy or delight the child but was, at best, a person who the child could trust to be there and care for them. He developed what is now called 'attachment theory', asserting that from very young, infants try to form a secure relationship to a reliable, caring adult. Separation from this carer is distressing to infants but when attachment is secure, the relationship becomes a base from which to explore the world around them.[17] Bowlby acknowledged that attachment did not necessarily need to be with

---

[15]   Anna Freud, Sigmund's daughter, also analysed children and did not accept Klein's theories. This led to a split between the 'London School' and the 'Viennese School'. Klein's theories were supported by the 'London School', which became the predominate model for psychoanalysis in Britain. The 'Viennese School' remained the stronger influence in USA.

[16]   In 1949, the World Health Organisation commissioned Bowlby to write a report on the mental health of homeless children in Europe. The resulting work, *Maternal Care and Mental Health*, was published in 1951, and in it he wrote '… the infant and young child should experience a warm, intimate, and continuous relationship with his mother (or permanent mother substitute) in which both find satisfaction and enjoyment'.

[17]   John Bowlby developed the theory of attachment and loss as outlined in a trio of books published between 1969 and 1982: *Attachment and Loss, vol. 1: Attachment*, New York: Basic Books, 1969; *Attachment and Loss, vol. 2: Separation*, New York: Basic Books, 1973; *Attachment and Loss, vol. 3: Loss, Sadness and Depression*, New York: Basic Books, 1980.

This is now an accepted way of understanding children's relationships to their caregivers. Secure attachments enable children to develop well.

one adult – there could be a few reliable carers – what mattered was their nearness and consistency in responding to the child.

Bowlby's theories were built on by the work of Mary Ainsworth and, later, by that of Daniel Stern.[18] They helped to establish, by careful observation of mothers and children, that the security of attachment is dependent on the *responsiveness* of the carer. As the psychologist Daphne de Marneffe points out, this is now an accepted view of the needs of infants and children:

> These widely validated patterns of attachment arise in the interaction of parent
> and child, and they reflect the impact of the parent's responses to the child's
> attachment-seeking behaviour ... When the caregiver's demands are in tune with
> fostering the baby's security and growth, things work out well for the baby.[19]

Bowlby's work established that an infant requires more than simply being fed and physically cared for; he needs a secure social relationship from the earliest period. Neglect or inconsistent and disorganised caring in the early years could lead to ongoing issues about relating to others in adulthood. Stern describes the way that this relationship develops at its best as attunement; mother and child tune themselves to each other, learning to read and understand the particularity of *this* mother and *this* child. Before exploring ideas about attachment and relationship further it is worth noting the work of another child development pioneer who stressed the importance of the mother/child relationship.

Winnicott – Being Good Enough

The paediatrician Donald Winnicott challenged the way that psychoanalysts focused on the child in isolation, saying there is 'no such thing as a baby' there is only a baby and a mother in a relationship. In observing mothers and children in healthy relationships he noted what he called 'maternal preoccupation' – a focusing on the baby so that the mother came to know and respond to *her particular* child. He referred to the concept of 'holding', which includes physical holding but encompasses far more. He wrote:

> It includes the whole routine of care throughout the day and night, and is not the
> same with any two infants because it is part of the infant, and no two infants are

---

[18]   Mary Ainsworth (1913–1999) was a developmental psychologist who worked on attachment theory and developed the strange situation procedure for assessing attachment in children. Daniel Stern is a professor of psychology specialising in the work of early childhood and is noted for *The Interpersonal World of the Infant*, New York: Basic Books, 1985.

[19]   Daphne de Marneffe, *Maternal Desire: On Children, Love and the Inner Life* (London 2006), p. 77.

alike. Also it follows the minute day-to-day changes belonging to the infant's growth and development, both physical and psychological.[20]

It is important to note here the particularity of each child, 'no two infants are alike' and the constantly changing nature of the infant. Winnicott *did* think that the ability to focus on the child was instinctual but, as we saw in the last chapter, to describe this process as instinctual seems to imply that it just happens. Naomi Stadlen, a modern observer of mothers and babies, maintains the way a mother learns about her child from simply holding him doesn't fit a definition of an instinct:

> They sit quietly for long stretches of time because this seems to keep their babies contented. It may feel like doing nothing at the time. But afterwards mothers realise that they have learned a great deal. It is often called 'instinctive knowledge' or 'intuitive knowledge' when the mother has acquired it. Perhaps this is because it is usually non-verbal and therefore *like* instinct and intuition. But instinct and intuition are quick reactions, whereas maternal understanding grows slowly.[21]

Winnicott's work has been important for maintaining that infants do not need a perfect response from their mothers. For the child to develop the capacity to do things for himself he needs to experience the times that a mother does not meet his needs. The fact that the mother did not always respond appropriately to the child was part of a healthy relationship. Mothers needed, he claimed, to be 'good enough' rather than perfect. That is, consistent enough in responding appropriately to the child but not always responding. The child could thus learn to trust that enough needs would be met but also learn that sometimes he needed to comfort himself:

> The good enough mother … starts off with an almost complete adaptation to her infant's needs, and as time proceeds she adapts less and less completely, gradually, according to the infant's growing ability to deal with her failure.[22]

His focus was on the perceived perception of the child and he still assumed a sense of merged identity between mother and child. A mother's failures enable the child to emerge into an understanding of his separate identity. His work stressed the importance of maternal care and acknowledged that it should be marked by continuity, reliability, graduated adaptation and 'provision for realising the child's

---

[20]   Donald Winnicott, *The Maturational Process and the Facilitating Environment* (London 1965), p. 49.

[21]   Stadlen, *What Mothers Do*, p. 93.

[22]   Donald Winnicott, *The Child, the Family and the Outside World* (London 1964), p. 44.

creative impulse'. With a good enough mother, he claimed, the infant will grow and eventually become a secure adult:

> Mothers with babies are dealing with a developing changing situation; the baby
> starts off not knowing about the world, and by the time they have finished their
> job the baby is grown up into someone who knows about the world and can find
> a way to live in it, and even to take part in the way it behaves, what a tremendous
> development.[23]

He acknowledges that mothers do not do this work alone; they, too, are part of a wider social network of support and care, and child-rearing can be a shared work. Yet what he is stressing is the centrality of a responsive caring relationship.

Benjamin – Inter-subjectivity

Important as the mother is in Winnicott's and Bowlby's theories, the relationship is viewed from the child's point of view with little exploration of what the mother gains from the relationship. The mother or carer is seen as one who plays a vital part in helping or hindering the child's attachment and sense of security. Yet assumptions that her part in this relationship is instinctual or intuitive, as we argued before, fail to credit her with an active role beyond the fulfilling of the necessary tasks. Jessica Benjamin's work is helpful in suggesting that this lack of interest in the mother's side of the relationship arises out of the continuing belief that the mother and baby have a merged sense of self. In *The Bonds of Love* she challenges accepted psychoanalytical ideas about a merged state arguing convincingly that this is not how most mothers view the relationship.[24] Winnicott had argued that mothers saw their baby as 'a bit of my own self'. Benjamin argues convincingly that a baby is not an extension of the mother's self; he is always recognised by her as a separate, albeit dependent, self. I would concur with this from my own experience and quote Stadlen's observations of babies and their mothers:

> Mothers and babies behave, from the start, as if they recognise each other as
> separate people … They may describe themselves and their babies as 'we', for
> example in a sentence like: 'We've had a really nice day together.' The whole
> point of this kind of sentence is that it describes two different people who are
> learning to understand each other and to get along. The mother's use of 'we'
> does not deny her baby's separateness, but affirms that they have found a way to
> be together nevertheless.[25]

---

[23]   Ibid., p. 69.

[24]   Benjamin, *The Bonds of Love*, p. 46–8.

[25]   Stadlen, *What Mothers Do*, p. 100.

Like Stadlen, Benjamin observes that mothers treat babies and children as others; unique individuals who show unique characteristics from the earliest days.[26]

Mothers are looking to build a relationship from the outset; they look for a response of recognition from the child:

> In this early interaction, the mother can already identify the first signs of mutual recognition: I recognise you as my baby who recognises me.[27]

> ...

> From the beginning there are always (at least) two subjects.[28]

Benjamin's view of mutual recognition is affirmed by the psychologist Daphne de Marneffe. In *Maternal Desire* she reflects on current research into the mother/child relationship:

> Contemporary researchers view babies and mothers as engaged in complex interactions from birth ... This mutual responsiveness of baby and caregiver, of self and other, runs throughout the baby's development ... An important theme underscored by this mother–infant research is that human psychological experience does not follow a linear progression from fusion to autonomy; rather, feelings of oneness and separateness oscillate throughout life.[29]

De Marneffe comments on the tendency to confuse the importance of attachment with psychoanalytical ideas of a merged state:

> It is important to distinguish between a baby's desire to *maintain proximity*, on the one hand, and his desire *to deny that the mother is a separate person*, on the other (if he indeed has such a desire), conflating them distorts how we see the mother's relationship to her child.[30]

---

[26] Although the experience of pregnancy is not necessary for good mothering, it can be argued that one of the ways it prepares women is through the complex reality of carrying another person in one's body. For most women, once the movement of the baby is felt, the reality of the otherness of the child is established. Mothers 'talk' to this other and assign characteristics to the movements. The sense that what is being carried in the body is not simply a part of the woman but is a person develops through pregnancy. It is, of course, only after birth that the reality of the person can be properly encountered, but the sense of separate subjectivity begins before that.

[27] Benjamin, *The Bonds of Love*, p. 15.

[28] Ibid., p. 24.

[29] de Marneffe, *Maternal Desire*, p. 67.

[30] Ibid., p. 69.

It also, I would argue, undermines the activity necessary from the mother in getting to know the child. A merged sense assumes that the mother has no need to actively seek to know her child and also perpetuates ideas that a mother is devastated by the child's desire to break this merged state and therefore tries to keep the child as a dependent infant. The reality is that mothers understand that an important aspect of fostering growth is allowing the child to move away while maintaining the ongoing security of attachment. In fact, modern observations of attachment in children find that those securely attached are more able to move freely between separation and closeness, trusting that they can rely on the comfort of their mother and other close caregivers when they need reassurance.

It is true that as children grow more adventurous and independent, mothers may experience a sense of loss as each developmental stage passes. Yet they usually delight to see their children grow and develop, gaining independence and taking their place in the wider world, often encouraging them on to the next stage. Most mothers will feel a sense of loss as some of the intimacy and intensity of the baby's needs are replaced by the more independent toddler and, eventually, by the teenager's need for his own space. Yet they will also be rejoicing in the freedoms that come as the child is less physically dependent; what mother doesn't rejoice in her child's faltering steps and take pleasure as he learns to walk, run and play? There are also immense pleasures as well as challenges as her child learns to talk and things can be discussed, negotiated and shared. My older children need far less physically, but now the demands draw on my ability to help them make sense of the complexity of life and emotions, to make choices for their future, and the pleasures come from their ability to be good company and, at times, a good source of support. The different stages of a child's development bring losses and gains, changes in the ways dependency is manifested and which needs the mother must attend to but it should be a mutually rewarding relationship for both.

Benjamin stresses that the relationship develops out of a growing mutual recognition and therefore needs to be understood as inter-subjective from the start. Two subjects are present thus challenging psychoanalytical assumptions about the necessity of finding subjectivity through separation:

> It [intersubjective theory] focuses, not on a linear movement from oneness to separateness, but on the paradoxical balance between them.[31]

Thus for a child to develop a healthy sense of self he needs to recognise the self that is his mother. The kind of games that are played across cultures and the ways a mother talks to her pre-lingual child all presuppose a mutuality and give and take.[32] Children learn to understand that there are similarities with the mother but also differences:

---

[31]   Benjamin, *The Bonds of Love*, p. 49.

[32]   Work has been done on studying the way mothers talk to their children before they develop speech. 'Motherese' has rhythmic musical patterns that can be seen across cultural

One of the most important insights of intersubjective theory is that sameness and difference exist simultaneously in mutual recognition. This insight allows us to counter the argument that human beings fundamentally desire the impossible absolutes of 'oneness' and perfection with the moderate view that things don't have to be perfect, that, in fact, it is better if they are not.[33]

This provides a more realistic and affirming language for mothers than Winnicott's use of the term 'failure'. In relationships, desires and expectations don't always coincide. From the earliest years, throughout a child's life, mother and child have to develop complex patterns of negotiation and compromise as the needs of each, and of other subjects in the broader family, are prioritised and met.

As human beings we are social and find value from social relationships. Benjamin argues that mutual relationships are satisfying to humans:

> But very early on we find that recognition between persons – understanding and being understood, being in attunement – is becoming an end in itself.[34]

It is true for the child and also for the mother. De Marneffe asserts that mothers can find their own sense of self and subjectivity enhanced through the relationship with her child. She is concerned that Benjamin implies that the mother's sense of subjectivity needs to be maintained by her willingness to leave her child; that her subjectivity is derived from outside the maternal relationship and needs to be, in some sense, protected from it:

> For the most part, Benjamin conceives a mother's independent identity in terms of those desires and aspirations that are distinct from her activities as caretaker for her child. She is not primarily concerned with how caring for children might express a woman's autonomous desires rather than thwart them.[35]

While acknowledging that experiences aside from mothering feed into and shape a mother's sense of self, de Marneffe argues that the experience of caring for children can itself be a means of developing a mother's sense of subjectivity. It is a relationship in which mothers can find purpose and meaning.

She acknowledges that child-rearing has been and may still be oppressive for women who feel they have no choice or little support. She also acknowledges that many aspects of domesticity have been elided with childcare in ways that are not helpful for articulating maternal work. Yet, she is concerned that challenging

---

and language differences. This involves communicating with the child, not simply talking at her. See de Marneffe, *Maternal Desire*, pp. 96–7.

[33] Benjamin, *The Bonds of Love*, p. 47.

[34] Jessica Benjamin, *Like Subjects, Love Objects: Essays on Recognition and Sexual Difference* (New Haven 1995), p. 32.

[35] de Marneffe, *Maternal Desire*, p. 75.

the way that motherhood can be oppressive has, in many instances, colluded in undervaluing and marginalising all that can be rewarding in maternal work. Looking again at research on attachment in infants she comments:

> In minutely describing the process by which mothers and babies together create a satisfying pattern of interaction, the research brings into focus some of the capacities that mothers bring to these interactions. And these capacities conform, in all relevant particulars, to the characteristics we commonly associate with a sense of self; the ability to reflect, to interpret, to enact goals, to respond flexibly and creatively, to share pleasure.[36]

In an interview discussing her book de Marneffe reiterates her view that it is in and through the relationship of care that mothers can find their subjectivity. I note, in the light of the previous chapter, that this involves resisting oppositional statements and finding new synthesised ways of viewing the world:

> The purpose of my book was to foreground the mother's experience of relatedness to her child. My essential point was that too often in discussions of motherhood, a woman's self-assertion and her care for others have been artificially placed in opposition. This doesn't capture the way that mothering puts women in a different subjective position, in that caring for their child and meeting the child's needs and desires often comes to be experienced as a way of meeting their own desire ... In other words, it is important not to limit our discussion of a mother's sense of self to those things she wants for herself apart from her baby. What she wants with and for her baby is integral to what she wants for herself. In some ways this is not a simple idea, because we are so used to either/or thinking: Either it's for the baby or it's for the mother. Both culturally and psychologically, it is so hard for us to stay in the realm of relatedness, to hold in tension the reality of two whole people, in a relationship.[37]

It is this sense of mothering as a rewarding, inter-subjective relationship that provides the basis for re-evaluating maternal work. It is a relationship that is aiming towards mutuality but it is also a relationship that is asymmetric, in which the child is dependent and in need of care:

When it is suggested that the development of the self is only possible by the rejection of the maternal, mothers are often characterised as those who want to maintain the dependency of their children, resisting their capacity to grow up. However, if mothering is understood as an on-going relationship of intersubjectivity, good enough mothers will find a way to balance the gains and losses inherent in nurturing a growing child so that he feels loved and supported

---

[36] Ibid., p. 76.

[37] 'Maternal Desire', an interview with Daphne de Marneffe, published on www. mothermovement.org (15 March 2011).

but not smothered. In a society where a mother's role is undervalued and where perhaps a woman is unsure about who she will be and what she will do once her children's need for her diminishes, it can be tempting for mothers to try to maximise their child's need of them into adulthood. This can lead to a manipulative need to be needed which is not part of good practice but is a result of a mother's lack of subjectivity. She has lost sight of the real child and is projecting her need to be needed onto the relationship, finding her validation in an inappropriate sense of ongoing control over the child's life. Such behaviour is most often associated with feelings of powerlessness in the wider context of life. I would conclude that it is a distortion of mothering for a mother to seek to infantilise her children, though it is a temptation, as Ruddick says, 'to depend emotionally on their children's dependence on them'.[38] To be needed by another can provide a powerful sense of validation and it must be acknowledged that this is a temptation in many caring relationships.

In mothering the stages of letting go and allowing a child to move on usually happen within a recognisable progression as the child grows up. Circumstances can and will mean that an older child needs more 'hands on' care at certain times. Illness and emotional traumas may make a child more dependent at a stage when they had been pretty independent. Yet on the whole there is a progression. Yet, this isn't a progression to autonomy but to more sophisticated patterns of interdependence in which adults give and receive care, moving between dependence and independence in all sorts of relationships. As the practical theologian Bonnie Miller-McLemore concludes:

> Human growth does not involve a movement from dependence to independence. Rather, growth entails learning more and more sophisticated modes of relating, with a movement from immature dependencies to more mature dependencies and attachments.[39]

I have argued, in this chapter, that mothering is not a simple outworking of a maternal instinct. Biology plays its part in why most women who have birthed children commit themselves to their ongoing care. The commitment to care for a child involves a process of learning and adapting to the needs of this child. This commitment is at best worked out in a relationship that looks for mutual recognition: that requires adaptation and negotiation between the two subjects of mother and child. Ideas of merged identity underplay the way that attachment develops relationally and diminishes a proper understanding of how even adults oscillate between experiences of dependence, independence and mutuality. The myth of the mother who wants to consistently infantalise her children needs to be challenged. Social and cultural attitudes to women and mothers may be responsible for such behaviour; it is not inherent in the practice of mothering.

---

[38] Ruddick, *Maternal Thinking*, p. 73.
[39] Bonnie Miller-McLemore, *Also a Mother* (Nashville 1994), p. 184.

Chapter 6
Mothering as a Practice

I have argued above that mothering cannot be understood as a simply instinctual response to a child but is a practice that needs to be learnt through an ongoing relationship of caring for that child. I have also suggested that the assumption of a maternal instinct has meant that the actual work of mothering has been under-articulated and undervalued. Before looking in more detail at the practice of mothering I will suggest that we find it a difficult practice to articulate because it does not fit into our modern ideas of work. To do this I will use Hannah Arendt's categories of labour, work and action. Another difficulty in talking about mothering is the concern that it involves asymmetric relationships of dependency. It is, therefore, a caring activity that raises issues about mutuality and reciprocity. To address these issues I will draw on Nel Noddings' work on the ethics of care and the luxury of time-limited relationships of dependency. This chapter will then look at Ruddick's concept of maternal practice, its cognitive capacities and virtues. By exploring these ideas I will offer a richer understanding of mothering that can in turn offer a more creative understanding of the practice of ministry.

Labour, Work and Action – Insights from Hannah Arendt

Mothering is both a physical process of caring, which inevitably involves a lot of mundane tasks, and a creative, meaningful activity. As I have already suggested it is both a relationship and an activity. It is, though, difficult to find a language to talk about what mothering entails without collapsing into functionalism. It is here and subsequently in our discussion of ministry that I find the work of the political philosopher Hannah Arendt helpful. Her definitions of human activity offer a framework which can help identify why mothering and ministry are so often seen as non-work or menial work. In *The Human Condition* she divides human activity into three categories. Labouring deals with the most immediate servicing of human needs, while work, or fabrication, provides the opportunities for making lasting objects and products. Finally, action is about human interaction – the possibilities of speech, relationships and politics – in the broadest sense of the word. I find it easiest to begin with her definition of work, perhaps because this is closest to the way society currently understands and values productive activity.

Work for Arendt is about the fabrication of things. She distinguishes between the 'work of our hands and the labour of our body'. It is skilled and is carried out under the guidance of a model or blueprint, which precedes the work and survives the work, enabling it to be used again for the fabrication of more products. This allows for multiplication, which she defines as very different from repetition. There is a beginning and an end, and the end is a product that has some kind of longevity and stability:

> To have a definite beginning and a definite, predictable end is the mark of fabrication, which through this characteristic alone distinguishes itself from all other human activities.[1]

Work is essentially individual or, as Arendt describes it, isolated, in that it needs an individual to design the blueprint and direct the work according to the model. Delegation is possible and often necessary; the craftsman may well involve others in carrying out aspects of the job under his direction; but it is very different from teamwork, which, Arendt claims, is both alien and 'destructive to workmanship'.[2] Work is about wresting things out of nature and about the end justifying the means:

> Here it is indeed true that the end justifies the means; it does more, it produces and organises them. The end justifies the violence done to nature to win the material, as the wood justifies killing the tree and the table justifies destroying the wood. Because of the end product, tools are designed and implements invented, and the same end product organises the work process ... everything is judged in terms of suitability and usefulness for the desired end, and for nothing else.[3]

The freedom for humans to work as fabricators involves others in engaging in labouring, for in contrast to work, labouring is about maintaining the necessities of life:

> The least durable of tangible things are those needed for the life process itself.[4]

> Whatever labour produces is meant to be fed into the human life process almost immediately, and this consumption, regenerating the life process, produces – or rather, reproduces – new 'labour power' needed for the further sustenance of the body.[5]

Labouring therefore needs to be understood as cyclical and repetitive. It also lends itself to being shared or, Arendt would say, it is collective. This means that individuals can pool their resources and can, when exhausted, pass on the tasks to another. They share the workload by adding their labour together or passing the burdens on. There are no blueprints in labouring, though there are clearly patterns

---

[1]   Hannah Arendt, *The Human Condition* (Chicago 1958; 2nd edn 1998), p. 144.
[2]   Ibid., p. 161.
[3]   Ibid., p. 153.
[4]   Ibid., p. 96.
[5]   Ibid., p. 99.

that can be followed, but these are open to modification. There is often no clear sense of where things begin and end. Anything produced is non-durable, or any kind of durability is incidental. The ongoing point of labouring is the sustenance of life and it is driven by necessity. Domestic work is labour, as is agriculture: both involve that repetitive, cyclical process aimed at keeping life going. Arendt points out that it is this area of activity that humans have, in the past, allocated to slaves or servants and therefore it is judged to be menial.

For Arendt, labouring is the lowest form of human activity and the highest form is action, which involves speech and the creation of webs of human relationships. It is in acting and speaking that humans explore both their unique distinctiveness and their plurality. Communities and webs of relationships develop through human action and the ability to talk about it. The telling of our own story and the interaction of that story with the stories of others is how we make sense of action, and of whom we are and who others are. These stories are 'not made up' and are in some sense intangible; they are the 'product' of action but are ongoing, unfinished, and they are always being shaped by new beginnings, new people who are born into the world. The two necessary components of action, according to Arendt, are the ability to forgive and the ability to make promises. This is because action is creative and contingent; there needs to be the ability to forgive mistakes and the willingness to trust others in order for communities and relationships to flourish. Action, Arendt reminds us, is about morality, about how we choose to act and how we make sense of our interactions. It is in our actions – our praxis – that relationships and communities are built up and politics in the widest sense of that term finds its place:

> Action, as distinguished from fabrication, is never possible in isolation; to be isolated is to be deprived of the capacity to act. Action and speech need the surrounding presence of others no less than fabrication needs the surrounding presence of nature for its material, and of a world in which to place the finished product. Fabrication is surrounded by and in constant contact with the world: action and speech are surrounded by and in constant contact with the web of the acts and words of other men.[6]

It is work or fabrication, she concludes, that offers the model of the autonomous, isolated man. Labouring involves unthinking cooperation and action involves the kinds of inter-subjective relationships central to this book.

As the analogy between mothering and ministry is explored in more detail in the subsequent chapters I will make use of Arendt's categories. But here it is important to note that mothering involves a mixture of labouring and action with very little work or fabrication. It is not involved with making a product. This is why ideas about work that value blueprints, formulas and measurable targets are unhelpful in assessing maternal practice and one of the reasons it is often

---

6   Ibid., p. 188.

undervalued. The labouring aspects are very apparent in the physical caring the child needs and these often overshadow the 'action': the meaningful activity of helping the child to develop their sense of being a person in relationship. It is easy to make a list of the tasks that are involved in the labouring aspects of mothering, but harder to articulate the action. This is why, as Stadlen suggests in her book title, much of what mothers do can 'look like nothing'.

Relationships of Care

This complex mixture of menial tasks and meaningful activity which is about relating to others rather than making products is apparent to some extent in all relationships of care. That is relationships where the aim is to serve and care for the needs of another. The ethicist and educational writer Noddings maintains that caring should be understood as a mutual, inter-subjective relationship despite the necessary asymmetry. She describes the two subjects as the one-caring and the one cared-for; they have different roles in the relationship, but both contribute. The one-caring is motivated by feelings for the other and these lead to action that involves attending to the other's needs. This 'feeling for the other' Noddings calls 'engrossment'. It involves recognising the subjectivity of the other and then making a temporary shift of focus from self to the other in what she calls a motivational displacement. There is thus in caring 'a moving away from self'; a 'disposability'.[7] But Noddings states 'one who is disposable recognises that she has a self to invest, to give ... She is *present* to the carer'. So this moving away from self is not about self-abnegation, but about a shift in focus. The one-caring focuses her *attention* on the one cared-for and the reality of her situation. I will look in more detail at the importance of attention when I explore Ruddick's *Maternal Thinking*. At this point it is worth noting that attending to the other is central to caring. Noddings writes:

> Caring involves stepping out of one's own personal frame of reference into the other's. When we care, we consider the other's point of view, his objective needs, and what he expects of us. Our attention, our mental engrossment is on the cared-for, not on ourselves.[8]

This attentive focus needs to be received by the cared-for who, in recognising the attitude of the one-caring, has the freedom to respond. Thus reception of caring is not passive but involves an active response. It is important that the one cared-for recognises that they are being treated as a subject and not as a problem, which would objectify them. In confirming that the one-caring has recognised the need

---

7   'Disposability, the readiness to bestow and spend oneself and make oneself available, and its contrary indisposability', quoted in Noddings, *Caring*, p. 19.

8   Ibid., p. 24.

and the reality of the other, the caring action can be received as care. This is the reciprocity in the relationship and is confirmed by the sense that the care given has been received in a way that helps or enhances the other. Noddings maintains that:

> What the cared-for gives to the relation either in direct response to the one-caring or in personal delight or in happy growth before her eyes is genuine reciprocity.[9]

Caring relationships are thus reciprocal but they are also asymmetrical. In order to maintain the reciprocity, the relationship needs to be *inter-subjective* despite the asymmetry. That means the one-caring needs a sense of their own self and an ability to recognise the feelings and needs of the other as a genuine subject. The moving away from self to focus on the other is a *temporary* process, a necessity of the particular act of caring, not a requirement of the ongoing relationship. Some relationships of care will mean that one person is most often in the role of the one-caring. This is true in mothering, where the dependence of the child shapes the balance of the caring, but this doesn't mean that the relationship is not mutual in the sense that each finds themselves recognised and enhanced through their interactions. Mothers do not have to lose their sense of self in meeting the needs of their dependent child. Noddings argues for a reappraisal of the way we view caring; seeing it as active, purposeful and rewarding. As I explore mothering and ministry further in this book I will draw on her ideas.

Practice and Virtue

To bring together these concepts of caring, labouring and action I will focus on Ruddick's *Maternal Thinking* and her understanding of mothering as a practice. Her motivation for writing is to show that the kind of caring activities that make up mothering are not antipathetic to reason and rationality but instead require particular ways of thinking and acting that shape good practice. Those mothering need to develop the capacity to think and act in concrete situations, deal with contingencies and maintain a secure, realistic relationship with a growing, developing, changeable human being. These ways of thinking and making decisions often do not conform to the kind of abstract reasoning that has been prioritised, but Ruddick argues that we need to value these different ways of thinking as appropriate and necessary for work that is focused on human relationships. One of the most important aspects of her work is the assertion that the demands of maternal work are all good but often not compatible. Thus it is necessary to hold together the reality of conflicting 'goods'. There are rarely definitively right answers. Instead, mothers constantly make judgements about what to prioritise; how to protect their child while helping him take the necessary risks for growth and development, and at the same time educate him about the limits and expectations of the society he is

---

[9]   Ibid., p. 74.

part of. Mothering is not about making products but about the action involved in helping unique human beings live out their own story.

To explore mothering Ruddick uses the philosophical terminology of a practice.[10] She describes how maternal practice is shaped by its threefold demands and that this requires the development of virtues.[11] Her understanding of virtue is basically Aristotelian so I will briefly outline his concept of virtue. In *Nicomachean Ethics* Aristotle defines virtues as the characteristics that enable a man to live a 'good' life. He maintains that actions are directed towards an end or *telos* and this end he defined as *eudaimonia*. A man needed to possess the virtues in order to achieve the end:

> The virtues are precisely those qualities the possession of which will enable an individual to achieve *eudaimonia* and the lack of which will frustrate his movement toward that *telos*.[12]

Virtues are necessary because many choices in life require judgement: choosing what is the right thing to do, at the right time, in the right way. It is not possible to achieve *eudaimonia* simply by applying a set of rules. Life is full of contingencies. Following rules may at times lead to good outcomes, but the individual will not necessarily have thought about or understood why they are good and may not be able to apply them in unusual circumstances. Virtues involve the ability to think about why something is appropriate, and develop a character that enables an individual to act virtuously again in different circumstances. Unlike rules with the concept of right or wrong, virtues involve finding the appropriate mathematical mean between two corresponding vices in a given situation. Thus courage is a mean between rashness and timidity, but finding this mean and understanding how to be courageous in a given situation is contingent on the concrete circumstances. What might be judged courageous in one setting may be seen as rash in another; the criterion for assessing the choice is not formulaic.

For Aristotle it is the intellectual virtue of *phronesis* that underpins contingent choice, enabling an individual to make the appropriate, virtuous response to particular circumstances. This virtue is intellectual but, because it deals with contingencies, it cannot be learned in abstract. It needs to be learned through experience and the ability to reflect on that experience; through practice. It is a way of thinking that is always associated with action, for the exercise of this virtue is about judging how to *act* appropriately in specific situations in order that these actions are in accordance with the overall aim, which in Aristotle's case was *eudaimonia*. *Phronesis* is concerned with the rightness of the means used to further the end and, as it is concerned with changeable and contingent situations,

---

10   Ruddick, *Maternal Thinking*, p. 14.

11   Ibid., p. 11.

12   Alasdair MacIntyre, *After Virtue* (London 1981; 3rd edn 2007), p. 148.

it is a necessary virtue in speaking about human interactions both in the household and in the wider community.

In revisiting Aristotle's ideas about virtue it is particularly worth noting this concept of virtue as a 'mean'. The tradition has developed – within the Church and beyond – of listing virtues alongside a list of vices or sins. This listing of contrary virtues and vices implies that virtue can be understood simply as an opposite to a sin or vice. Thus humility is often understood as the virtue contrary to pride. However, the concept of opposites loses the subtlety of an Aristotelian 'mean' and can lead to a mistaken assumption that anything contrary to pride is thus humility. As Alastair MacIntyre says of Aristotle's definition of virtues:

> For each virtue therefore there are two corresponding vices. And what it is to fall into a vice cannot be adequately specified independently of circumstances: the very same action which would in one situation be liberality could in another be prodigality and in a third meanness. Hence judgement has an indispensable role in the life of the virtuous man which it does not and could not have in, for example, the life of the merely law-abiding or rule-abiding man.[13]

When we return to Ruddick's use of virtue we will see that she understands this Aristotelian mean. Each of the virtues that she identifies in the practice of mothering is explored alongside what she terms its 'degenerate forms'.

For Aristotle, the good end of a man's life, the *telos*, was expressed as a universal aim. However, it was not open to all; his particular worldview meant that only the free, educated man was capable of living in such a way. In revisiting Aristotle's virtues, the philosopher MacIntyre retains a teleological understanding, but sets that within the concept of human practices. In living a life that aims to be good, people may be engaged in a number of practices. Each practice has a *telos*; the *telos* is purposeful, but may be specific to the practice. It follows that there can be different practices aiming at different particular 'goods', with different equally valuable aims. In each case the practice provides the background and context for the 'good', and allows for the possibility of conflicting goods.

Aristotle's position assumed that conflict arose out of failures in virtue that were character flaws. MacIntyre suggests that by understanding the possibility of multiple good practices conflict is not necessarily a failure or sign of a flawed character. This means that conflict can arise out of the demands of different practices and competing 'goods'. Conflict can thus be part of the process of honing a practice. As noted above, Ruddick goes further than this and says that conflicting goods are actually internal to the practice of mothering. The tension between competing goods is a defining aspect of the practice which has as its *telos* the child's maturity. It is because of these tensions and the need to make contingent choices about which good to prioritise that maternal practice requires virtues rather than rules.

---

[13]   Ibid., p. 154.

Practices and their virtues arise out of a living tradition shaped and informed by other practitioners. An individual's practice develops through participation in an ongoing 'argument' or conversation about what is good practice. Thus understanding and making good choices about how to act is inherently social. It follows that the virtues of mothering are learnt through practice and through the reflection on that practice that arises from the speaking and reflecting on mothering with others who are engaged in bringing up children or who have done so in the past. At its best mothering should be an inherently social practice.

Mothering as a Practice

The practice of mothering shapes the relationship of care in which a child or children grow to maturity. It aims, in MacIntyre's terms, to enable children to develop the capacity to think and act virtuously as independent practical reasoners.[14] For Ruddick, the starting point is the three constituent demands. The first of these is to preserve the life of the child which involves keeping a child safe, meeting its physical needs and can be characterised by 'holding'. The second is to 'nurture its emotional and intellectual growth' which involves broadening the child's world, allowing him to take risks, to explore and consequently can be characterised by letting go. Ruddick's third demand is more complex and, as she notes, is made not by the needs of the child 'but by the social groups of which a mother is a member'. Ruddick calls this acceptability: the aim of a mother to bring up a child who can find a secure place in the world of the family and the world beyond the family.

These demands, Ruddick claims, require disciplined ways of thinking, even if many mothers would not use this terminology. At times, as I have already noted, these demands conflict. To keep a child safe means minimising risk, while to foster growth means allowing risk-taking. To foster growth means to encourage the pushing of boundaries, but to maintain acceptability means helping the child to recognise where certain boundaries exist. To preserve a child's unique identity may mean challenging social norms on behalf of the child and even challenging the mother's own set of beliefs and values. These issues present the one mothering with constant choices shaped by the question: What is the best thing for this child, at this moment, in this situation? She is dealing with contingencies and needs to act appropriately both contextually and within the wider understanding of what it is to be a good, or 'good enough', mother. Even though, in many cases, these thoughts may not be clearly articulated, Ruddick maintains that they can be understood as a discipline of thought particular to the demands of mothering. This discipline she suggests:

---

[14]   Alastair MacIntyre, *Dependent Rational Animals: Why Human Beings Need the Virtues* (London 1999), ch. 8, pp. 81–99.

establishes criteria for determining failure and success, sets priorities, and identifies virtues that the discipline requires. Like any other work, mothering is prey to characteristic temptations that it must identify.[15]

Ruddick constantly asserts, to name the virtues is not to claim to possess them but to begin to articulate the complex temptations and virtues that are part of maternal practice. Clearly, there will always be cultural differences in aspects of what is understood as good mothering; however, Ruddick claims, and I agree, the demands she outlines can be understood across cultural differences. All mothers need to fulfil these demands within their cultural context. As Noddings comments:

> Suppose we start with Ruddick's maternal interests … A maternal figure (female or male) must respond to three great demands (or needs) of the child: preservation, growth, and acceptability. These needs are both practical and universal, but their explication – their filling out – involves us in personal, cultural, and practical complexities.[16]

Ruddick's language of maternal practice and associated virtues offers a way of articulating how mothers aim to respond appropriately to their children in the concrete situations of everyday life. She is affirming that maternal practice involves ways of reasoned thinking and acting and cannot be described in formulaic language. This ability to act well contingently is akin to the Aristotelian virtue of *phronesis*. Ruddick does not use this terminology. She does, however, write about judging tenderly and learning to reflect through developing conscientiousness. Such conscientious responsiveness requires ways of thinking that are different from practices which would fit more easily into Arendt's work model. It requires *phronesis* or, as Jean Porter translates it, prudence:

> The prudent person applies moral rules through a process of judgement rather than employing a decision procedure similar to that of a mathematician, because *there is no other way to apply rules* of this kind.[17]

This contrast between prudent judgement and formulaic rules does not imply an insufficiency in the former, but affirms that when dealing with contingent singulars, the certainty of maths is not an option.

It also follows that acting well in contingent circumstances involves the capacity to think in concrete ways. I noted, when looking at issues of gender, that those who assert differences between men and women suggest that women tend to think concretely rather than abstractly. Gilligan's work on moral decision-making made this very point. Yet, rather than posit essentialist gender differences, it makes

---

[15] Ruddick, *Maternal Thinking*, p. 24.

[16] Nel Noddings, *Starting at Home* (Berkeley 2002), p. 62.

[17] Jean Porter, *Moral Action and Christian Ethics* (Cambridge 1995), p. 150.

sense to suggest that the generalisation about women's more concrete thinking is connected to the caring roles that have more often been assumed by women, particularly child-rearing. These roles call for concrete thinking not because it is 'better' than abstract thinking in any definable sense, or because women are not capable of abstract thinking, but because it is the *appropriate* way of thinking to sustain a caring practice such as mothering with all the contingent choices it involves. As Ruddick comments:

> A child's acts are irregular, unpredictable, often mysterious … A mother who took one day's conclusions to be permanent or invented sharp distinctions to describe her child's choices would be left floundering. The virtues of abstraction and concrete cognition vary with the contexts of thinking.[18]

Thus we can conclude that in terms of an ongoing human relationship of nurturing care, abstract thinking is often neither appropriate nor sustainable. Concrete ways of decision-making, prudent judgements, are necessary to a practice that, because it deals with human relationships, always requires a contextual approach. This is true for mothering and in the following chapter I will argue it is also true for parish ministry. Both practices deal with the complexity of caring for real people in real situations. Abstract ideas may offer helpful insights but must always be contextualised by the concrete realities of particularity and contingency.

Children are constantly growing and developing and mothering requires the ability to respond to this child at this stage of life. To do this mothers need what Ruddick calls the cognitive capacity and virtue of attentive love. She draws on Iris Murdoch's *The Sovereignty of Good* to define this attention.[19] Murdoch borrows the concept of attention from Simone Weill and defines it as really seeing the reality of the other and not the fantasy that we so easily project. Murdoch connects this to love:

> It is in the capacity to love, that is to *see*, that the liberation of the soul from fantasy consists. The freedom which is a proper human goal is the freedom from fantasy, that is the realism of compassion. What I have called fantasy, the proliferation of blinding self-centred aims and images, is itself a powerful system of energy, and most of what is often called 'will' or 'willing' belongs to this system. What counteracts the system is attention to reality inspired by, consisting of, love.[20]

This attention is akin to Noddings' ideas about engrossment and motivational displacement: a moving from self-centredness to really focus on the subjectivity of the other, to see them as themselves:

---

[18]   Ruddick, *Maternal Thinking*, p. 96.

[19]   Iris Murdoch, *The Sovereignty of Good* (London 1970), p. 34.

[20]   Ibid., p. 67.

Apprehending the other's reality, feeling what he feels as nearly as possible, is the essential part of caring from the view of the one-caring. For if I take on the other's reality as possibility and begin to feel its reality, I feel, also, that I must act accordingly; that is, I am impelled to act as though in my own behalf, but in behalf of the other.[21]

Ruddick builds on the way that Murdoch relates *attention* to both reality and love. She describes attentive love as the overarching virtue that 'knits together' maternal thinking. Reflecting on Weil's description of the Grail legend in which the defining question to the suffering knight[22] is 'What are you going through?' Ruddick writes:

The ordinary secular mother also learns to ask 'what are you going through?' and to wait to hear the answer rather than giving it. She learns to ask again and keep listening even if she cannot make sense of what she hears or can barely tolerate the child she has understood. Attention is akin to empathy … However, the idea of empathy, as it is popularly understood, underestimates the importance of knowing another *without* finding yourself in her.[23]

Noddings makes a similar point, stressing that empathy carries with it the idea of recognising one's own feelings in the feelings of another so that one can feel with them.[24] She prefers the word 'sympathy' and Ruddick, 'compassion'. Both terms convey the idea that we recognise and feel with the other even when their feelings are not like our own. In both cases what they are stressing is the ability to attend to and feel with another by focusing on who they are and what their situation is at that moment.

In the earlier discussion of attachment I stressed the importance of attending to the real child, getting to know this particular child. This is described by some writers as attunement; the recognition between a particular mother and child that is necessary for secure attachment. It is mainly emphasised in the early years, but it continues to be important as the child develops and grows, requiring continuing attention and attunement to the changing reality. As Ruddick argues it takes a level of *discipline* to see the child as he is, not as you might like him to be or fear he may be. Following Murdoch's thinking we note that this involves letting go of the fantasy child who comes from our own expectations of how the child should be, how others describe him and from the descriptions of other people's children or

---

[21] Noddings, *Caring*, p. 16.

[22] Simone Weil, the philosophical and mystical writer, discusses 'attention' in connection to the Grail legend in 'Reflections on the Right Usage of School Studies in View of the Love of God', in *Waiting on God*, translated from the French by Emma Crauford (London 1977), pp. 53–61.

[23] Ruddick, *Maternal Thinking*, p. 121.

[24] For a fuller discussion see Noddings, *Caring*, pp. 30–32.

those described in the childcare literature. Gerhardt describes the responsiveness such attention requires, finding an appropriate mean between neglect, ignoring his needs and over-intrusive care; meeting needs the baby hasn't actually expressed but the mother projects on to him. She writes:

> Researchers have refined our knowledge to the point where we can now say that babies need not too much, not too little but just the right amount of responsiveness – not the kind that jumps anxiously to meet their every need, nor the kind that ignores them for too long, but the kind of relaxed responsiveness that confident parents tend to have ... What is more, the best responsiveness for babies is the 'contingent' kind. This means that the parents need to respond to the actual needs of their particular baby, not to their own idea of what a baby might need ... Each baby needs a tailor-made response, not an off-the-shelf kind, however benign ... Each situation requires its own appropriate, contingent response, suitable for the personality of this particular baby.[25]

Such appropriate responsiveness requires a proper assessment of the place of feelings in acting well. Feelings can often be dismissed as antithetical to reason, but in mothering, and in all caring, feelings need to be taken seriously and there needs to be a better understanding of how some kinds of reasoning utilise and value feelings. In describing caring Noddings states, 'We do not begin by formulating or solving a problem but by sharing a feeling.'[26] And it is at this level of feeling that we relate to the other. She goes on to say 'Feeling is not *all* that is involved in caring, but it is essentially involved.'[27]

There has often been a false dichotomy between reasoned thinking and emotional feelings. Ruddick maintains that mothering challenges this dichotomy requiring instead a synthesis of reason and feeling in which feelings are the basis on which reasoned action is both enacted and evaluated. She describes 'reflective feeling' as 'one of the most difficult attainments of reason'. In caring for a child, Ruddick maintains, it is the feelings aroused by the child's needs that prompts first reflection and then action. The action is then evaluated by reflecting on the feelings of child and mother.[28] The importance of utilising feelings to motivate and evaluate action means that such action cannot be rule-based. Instead mothers use feelings and reason to reflect on the practice in a way that at its best develops appropriate maternal virtues. The virtues that Ruddick names help mothers meet the demands of the practice, guard against the temptations and choose wisely, again and again, how to respond to the contingent needs of their particular child. They are characteristics developed through the practice and the reflection on the practice. A reflection that is attentive, feeling and motivated by love.

---

25 Gerhardt, *Why Love Matters*, p. 197.
26 Noddings, *Caring*, p. 31.
27 Ibid., p. 32.
28 Ruddick, *Maternal thinking*, p. 72.

Ruddick's Maternal Thinking

In describing maternal practice Ruddick names certain virtues and their degenerate forms; that is the temptation, often for seemingly good reasons, to move either side of the mathematical mean into a way of acting that is not life-giving. For example we noted in Gerhardt's quote above that over-intrusive care or the degeneration into neglect are both temptations of mothering which distort the demand to care for the child and through this distortion can fail to enable the mother and child to flourish. Ruddick's concept of degenerative forms of the virtues, and the temptations faced by mothers to fall into these forms, provides an insightful way of looking at best practice.

We can see this in Ruddick's discussion of the maternal virtue of humility. The first and, Ruddick would claim, most basic demand of mothering is to preserve the life entrusted to her care. However, this presents the mother with complex questions about what can and cannot be controlled in order to keep a child safe. Mothers must contend both with the independent will of the child and the many uncontrollable aspects of the world in which they live. The reality is that they cannot control everything in order to protect the child and the temptation to do so can lead to the kind of intrusive care that stifles growth. This leads Ruddick to identify humility as a primary maternal virtue. Humility enables a mother to understand that she cannot control everything in a child's life to keep it safe. It enables her to understand her own limitations, the freedom of the child and the complexity of the world he inhabits.

Notwithstanding all that is beyond her control, a mother, she argues, cannot simply relinquish control. The virtue of humility helps her to find the balance between an excessive control and a passive abnegation. For Ruddick the virtue of humility is linked to the mother's recognition of the subjectivity of the child, 'the independent, uncontrollable will of the other'.[29] The temptations, the degenerate forms, of the virtue of humility are either to domination – asserting the mother's will regardless of the child, or a submissive passivity in which she is dominated by the child or by the expertise of others. In terms of the wider world beyond her control the temptation is to try to limit all risk or to despair and relinquish control to others or simply abnegate responsibility. In describing humility Ruddick again draws on Murdoch, who describes humility as a 'selfless respect for reality and one of the most difficult and central of virtues'. She notes that a sense of despair and powerlessness may mean that humility degenerates into a kind of self-effacement, 'rather like having an inaudible voice.'[30]

The temptations of domination and passivity are the same ones that Benjamin identifies as arising out of a breakdown in inter-subjectivity between mother and child. Domination is a result of a fantasy, but that does not mean it stems initially from wrong motivation. For the mother, as Ruddick notes, it is the fantasy of

---

[29] Ibid., p. 72.
[30] Murdoch, *Sovereignty of Good*, p. 95.

perfect control often motivated by an overwhelming desire to keep the child safe. For the child, domination may arise out of a mistaken belief that he can move beyond any kind of dependency. In both cases there is a tendency to move from relationships of mutuality and interdependence towards assertion of one will over the other. Passivity is also a failure in inter-subjectivity; the inability to take responsibility for what is within one's control may arise because of a lack of self-belief. The mother's motivation to protect is good but it needs to be tempered by letting go of the fantasy of perfect protection and acknowledging all that is beyond her control, the reality of chance, unpredictability and the independent will of the other. Ruddick writes:

> Mothers protect where protection cannot be assured, where failure usually means disappointing someone they passionately love, where chance and unpredictable behaviour limit their efforts, and where their best efforts are flawed by their own impatience, anxiety, fatigue, and self-preoccupation.[31]

In order to cope with this unpredictability mothers need to cultivate the virtue of cheerfulness. Ruddick draws on Spinoza for her choice of cheerfulness as a maternal virtue. It is a less familiar word for a virtue but, I suggest, can be seen as akin to the theological virtue of hope, though in Ruddick's secular view it has nothing to do with the divine. She talks about it as the positive attitudes mothers develop in order to keep on caring for their child and rejoicing in doing so, despite acknowledging the complex realities of the world.

The degenerate forms of this virtue are 'cheery denial' or despair. Cheery denial is another form of fantasy in which the dark and difficult is denied either in the mothers experience of caring or in what she allows the child to explore. Such denial represses complex emotions and fails to enable children to understand and explore the more difficult feelings and experiences. The virtue of cheerfulness enables mothers to resist both this denial of the difficulties of life and, on the other hand, the lack of hope that leads to despair. In doing so, Ruddick claims, they aim to confront reality with 'resilient clear-sightedness' and here she does use the word hope:

> To be cheerful is to see a child hopefully and to welcome her hopes; for children, hope is as important as breathing.[32]

This hope, and ongoing belief in the possibilities of and for the child, is connected to what she calls a mother's double focus. This is an ability to be immersed in the here and now but always with a larger vision; a 'simultaneous, or at least rapidly shifting, double focus on small and great, near and eternal'. These virtues of humility and cheerfulness are necessary in mothering throughout the child's changing life. As we noted above she characterises preservative love as 'holding':

---

[31]   Ruddick, *Maternal Thinking*, p. 73.
[32]   Ibid., p. 74.

'To hold means to minimise risk and to reconcile differences'. This way of being is a necessity from the earliest days of a baby through to protecting and preserving the lives of teenage boys. Understanding the reality of what is controllable and practising the virtues of humility and clear-sighted cheerful hope involves the ongoing struggle to resist the temptations to domination or despairing abnegation of responsibility.

Following on from, but often in tension with, the demand to preserve the child's life is the demand to foster growth and to 'nurture a child's unfolding, expanding material spirit'.[33] She maintains that the central tasks of fostering growth are 'administrative'. They revolve around creating a home and organising the places and times for socialising beyond the home:

> Whatever its' particular structure, a home is the headquarters for a mother's organising and a child's growing. Home is where children are supposed to return when their world turns heartless, where they centre themselves in the world they are discovering.[34]

Fostering growth requires a welcoming attitude to change and the capacity to think concretely in ways discussed above. It involves the capacity to let 'a child grow into her life – which also means growing away'. Thus we see that it can often be in tension with the desire to protect. The holding aspect of mothering discussed above needs to be tempered with this ability to let children go and grow to ensure that holding does not become clinging. Yet, as Ruddick suggests, there is a responsibility on the part of the mother to resource the child for his explorations in the world. One of the ways she suggests that mothers do this is through storytelling; narrating a child's own life and setting that within the stories and narratives of other lives.

This storytelling requires the recognition of subjectivity. Stories help the child to understand that their life has a coherence that is ongoing and can be narrated, but that their story is just one of many in which others are also subjects. MacIntyre describes subjectivity thus:

> To be the subject of a narrative that runs from one's birth to one's death is … to be accountable for the actions and experiences which compose a narratable life … The narrative of any one life is part of an interlocking set of narratives. Moreover, this asking for and giving of accounts itself plays an important part in constituting narratives.[35]

Both MacIntyre and Ruddick maintain that a child learns how to make sense of his own narrative through conversations and storytelling. Thus mothering involves

---

[33] Ibid., p. 83.
[34] Ibid., p. 87.
[35] MacIntyre, *After Virtue*, p. 217.

telling stories and listening to the child's stories and accounts of life. MacIntyre maintains that children need stories which help them reflect on their own lives. They also need to hear stories that challenge their perceptions and help them to imagine different futures and outcomes. Thus children need fictional stories to fire the imagination and posit alternative realities, as well as the narration of the children's and families real lives. Ruddick claims that storytelling at its best 'enables children to adapt, edit and invent life stories of their own'.[36]

She also points out that it is through the storytelling inherent in conversations with other mothers, and others who are concerned for the child, that mothers develop ways of thinking and narrating their own practice. As they narrate the experiences of their mothering to others, they can begin to reflect on the practice. Maternal stories allow mothers to describe the particularities of their children in ways that elicit others sympathy, amusement or respect. They also help them find coherence in what may have been confusing or frightening episodes. I would also note that an interesting feature of the stories mothers tell each other about their children is the way that failures are shared as collective wisdom. Ruddick comments that isolated mothers do not benefit from a collective experience in which the stories told can be 'collectively judged and improved'. She is concerned that social pressures that lead to a lack of time for maternal chatting make it harder for mothers to help their children learn to narrate their own life and appreciate the complexity of the lives of others.

It is in the context of maternal storytelling that Ruddick notes a set of maternal virtues: realism, compassion and delight. We have already seen how realism is a central aspect of attentive love and of cheerfulness. In the context of maternal storytelling, realism is the virtue that guards against a falsely cheerful over-editing or an uncaring and inappropriate confrontation with aspects of the adult world. A mother's storytelling must be trustworthy and deal with the complexity of life and its range of emotions but told with care and concern for the child. This is why mothers need to cultivate the virtue of compassion. Ruddick links compassionate storytelling to the capacity to forgive; 'to forgive themselves as they have been forgiven'.[37]

Here again we find Ruddick using language that relates to theological ideas, connecting compassion with the capacity to forgive and to be forgiven. It is also interesting to note Arendt's use of the same concept. In her account of action, which connects to the ability to speak and interact through speech and storytelling she, like Ruddick, identifies the capacity to forgive and to be forgiven. Both writers acknowledge that human interaction is fraught with the possibilities of not reading the other right or responding inappropriately and, as Arendt comments, forgiveness enables us to move on. I will return to these ideas in the next chapter in the context of parish ministry.

---

[36]　Ruddick, *Maternal Thinking*, p. 98.

[37]　Ibid., p. 100.

Alongside realism and compassion, Ruddick links this narrative task to 'delight', which she describes as a virtue and a discipline. In her definition delight involves shared pleasure and an ability to respond to the child's pleasures, which may well be very different from one's own. She talks about delight as a disciplined response, learning to appreciate the interests and achievements as children grow and become themselves.[38] At times it may be easy to delight in the interests of one's child but there will be things that to the mother seem insignificant or frankly uninteresting which need to be understood and valued from the child's perspective. Hours on a cold touchline learning to delight in my son's ability to play football, a game I do not fully understand, has been a discipline and a joy.

Ruddick suggests that the virtues of realism, compassion and delight need to be cultivated to guard against many temptations:

> As they talk to and about their children, mothers often fail to resist many temptations: they deny their own confusion and children's failure, punish or pity rather than sympathise, manipulate or prematurely console rather than speak truthfully, delight too half-heartedly and too late out of self-preoccupation or perfectionism. If mothers count realism, compassion and delight as virtues of the stories they tell, then they recognise and set themselves to resist such temptations.[39]

Clearly, I would add, this storytelling is not done by the mother alone. Children learn to hear and enjoy stories from other sources, learn to narrate their own lives through talking to others. Yet it is an important aspect of mothering. The consistency and familiarity of the mother and child means, at best, that the mother becomes a trustworthy narrator and listener, helping her child make meaning out of the complexity of their own and others' lives.

Ruddick's third demand of 'acceptability' is the most contested. It involves teaching, training or educating a child to take her place within the wider society, passing on values and shaping a moral character. Mothers are aiming to bring up a child who they like and who they feel others will accept and appreciate. This area is contentious because it raises issues about how one instils moral or religious values and whether children learn best through strict routines or more fluid discipline. It will be clear from earlier discussions that Ruddick is not primarily interested in routines that teach a child to conform but the more complex issue of how to instil conscientiousness in one's child. Again it is worth noting that this correlates to MacIntyre's description of a 'mature practical reasoner'. As Ruddick says, the hope is that you raise a child who behaves well when you are not there and in circumstances you do not control. This education or training of a child is, Ruddick

---

[38] Ibid.
[39] Ibid., p. 101.

suggests, a double work of conscience. The mother's conscientiousness provides a model for the developing conscientiousness of the child.[40]

It follows therefore that a mother has to develop the capacity for self-reflection as she teaches her child to reflect. She also needs to accept the possibility of her own values and beliefs being challenged. In order to foster conscientiousness mothers need to practice authenticity and the virtue of 'proper trust'. Ruddick identifies the degenerate forms of this virtue as unquestioning obedience or blind trust. She acknowledges that a mother will not always get things right and will sometimes let her child down but she has a responsibility to be trustworthy enough for the child to rely on her.[41] She must also learn to trust her children and guard against the temptations to constantly suspect the worst or to be too trusting, failing to name what is not acceptable. Ruddick goes on to say that this trust between mother and child is, like other virtues, a constant balancing act, avoiding the temptation to demand blind obedience or to fail to name what is wrong. This proper trust connects to Arendt's argument that the ability to make and keep promises is a necessary component of action. Again, I will explore this more fully in connection with parish ministry. I simply note at this point how Ruddick's maternal practice connects to Arendt's realm of action.

We saw earlier that Aristotle identified the virtue of *phronesis* as the intellectual capacity to act virtuously in contingent circumstances. Ruddick does not use the term, but she talks about developing the capacity to 'judge tenderly yet with confidence'. This is learned through attending to the child, practising compassion, being able to feel with the other, and trying to understand them even if we do not ourselves comprehend their pain or confusion. It also involves the virtues of realism and delight. It is an ongoing process and, as mothers develop their own sense of what it is to be virtuous, they are simultaneously engaged in teaching their children how to be virtuous. They need to judge tenderly but well in order to find the difficult balance between instilling their own values in their children while allowing the children to question, challenge and posit alternatives so that they become morally mature as themselves. It is, I would say, one of the delights of parenting when your children act unprompted in ways that show their conscientiousness to others. The temptation to insist too strongly on conforming to the mother's deeply held values or of giving in too lightly to their challenges are real temptations that mothers need to guard against. Ruddick suggests that experiencing guilt and shame at times is a necessary part of developing conscientiousness:[42] Thus we note again the importance of forgiveness, of seeing failures as opportunities to develop wisdom and of teaching children to make amends and to start again.

---

[40]   Ibid., p. 117.

[41]   Ibid., p. 118.

[42]   Ibid., p. 109.

Ruddick's book is titled *Maternal Thinking*[43] but she concludes her discussion of this thinking, which I have summarised above, by pointing out that mothering is about doing. Mothers attend to their children in order to respond to them and do for them what is necessary for their flourishing.[44] By beginning with thinking, Ruddick has challenged perceptions about mothers simply reacting to their children in some instinctual way or that child-rearing is unskilled and irrational work. Instead it is possible to affirm that in order to raise children mothers, and others who engage in mothering, need to develop capacities to respond appropriately in contingent circumstances. They need to constantly adapt to a changing individual, altering the kinds of care and involvement required. They need to help children make sense of a complex world and come to terms with their own and others' failings. Ruddick makes a compelling case that this involves developing ways of reasoning and recognising virtues that can help a mother act well. As she points out, to identify a virtue is not to possess it, but in finding ways of articulating the temptations and struggles it helps to reflect on the practice and the aim of being good enough.

[43]   The first two parts of *Maternal Thinking* deal with Ruddick's exploration of maternal practice. The final part uses a 'maternal standpoint' to reflect on peace and the politics of war.

[44]   Ruddick, *Maternal Thinking*, p. 123.

PART III
Mothering as a Metaphor for Ministry

Chapter 7
Using Mothering to Think about Ministry

At the end of the first chapter I concluded that to be a parish priest was to take on the responsibility of care for a particular community of people. I also argued that the role of the priest needed to be understood as a relationship. In the subsequent chapters I have looked at the particular relationship of care that is mothering, challenging ideas about instinctual care and exploring the ways in which those mothering have to learn to think and respond appropriately. I noted the importance of inter-subjectivity despite the asymmetry of the relationship. I will now use the insights from mothering to look at the role of a parish priest. The aim is to find a way of articulating good practice that takes seriously both the being and doing of clergy.

Priests, of course, carry out their ministry in a number of different settings. Some are based as chaplains in different kinds of sector ministry. Some are combining secular jobs with parish ministry, offering different amounts of time depending on circumstances. Those engaged in parish ministry may have the care of one church and one parish or a number of different buildings, communities, parishes and responsibilities. In this book the focus is specifically on the work of a parish priest, envisaging someone who has received the cure of souls for a particular parish or group of parishes. I hope that those whose priesthood is carried out in a different set of relationships can draw insights from what I am saying, but I know from my own experience that the relationship of a chaplain to the community she serves is different at certain levels from that of a vicar. It is therefore important to understand the context of priestly ministry being discussed. Many of the books on ministry try to cover all aspects of priestly ministry and thus fail to provide a grounded picture of contextual practice.

In mothering there are tensions over the terminology used about 'full' or 'part-time' work and we find similar difficulties in talking about ordained ministry. Discussions around the terminology of 'working' and stay-at-home mothers have parallels with how we speak about those who are not engaged in full-time stipendiary ministry. How we find a better language and appreciate the complexities of different working patterns and relationships for non-residential clergy, or those whose primary work is elsewhere, is an important task for the wider Church. However, they are not questions that I can explore in this book. So, for the purpose of this piece of work, when I talk about a priest I am particularly thinking of an incumbent; the language I use will reflect on relating to a parish and I hope those who care for many will be able to translate this into a large, vibrant family of parishes.

The Demands Shaping the Practice of Parish Ministry

If parish ministry is to be understood as a practice then it is important to identify the demands that shape the practice. The ordinal describes the role of a priest in a mixture of overarching aims and practical tasks. Priests have a responsibility for others, principally for 'the community of faithful' who are to be nurtured and sustained, fed, taught and admonished so that 'we all may grow into the fullness of Christ'. They also have a wider responsibility for the 'family' of the Lord, which includes both those who are involved in the Church and those beyond. They are to guide people, care for them, foster their gifts and, above all, build up the Church. The sacraments are to be used to sustain and nurture the community of faith, as well as to proclaim the mighty acts of God and tell His story in the world. The overarching aim can be summarised as a ministry through which the people of God, in the widest sense of the term, are helped to grow into 'the fullness of Christ and be a living sacrifice presentable to God'.[1]

It is interesting to note that the terminology used in the phrase above can be found in New Testament passages that list the variety of ministries in the church. Ephesians 4:13–14 describes growing up into 'the measure of the full stature of Christ'[2] and Romans 12:1 exhorts 'presenting our bodies as living sacrifices'. John Muddiman, commentating on the passage in Ephesians writes:

> Christ's gift of ministries in the Church is intended to enable Christians to achieve a mature faith measured by the full stature of Christ himself.[3]

This, then, offers an insight into the calling of clergy: they are to sustain and help all of the Church to grow up, to develop a mature faith. This is clearly about both individuals and the corporate life of the Church. It is, therefore, possible to conclude that the gifts of ministry are given because Christians need to grow up spiritually within relationships and communities that nurture and foster that growth. If shaping and sustaining such relationships and communities is at the heart of the calling of the ordained then the demands of the practice will reflect this. Looking at the practice of mothering has enabled reflection on the kind of relationships and environment in which human beings ordinarily grow up and mature. We have seen that committed, attentive, responsive relationships provide the best environment for humans to become mature and flourish. It follows that similar relational responsiveness will provide the best environment for Christians

---

[1]   These phrases are used in the Common Worship service for the Ordination of Priests.

[2]   Ephesians 4:13–14 describes this aim of maturity measured by the full stature of Christ. Tom Wright, in *Virtue Reborn* (London 2010), explores this concept of Christian maturity, linking it to an Aristotelian idea of virtuous living.

[3]   John Muddiman, *The Epistle to the Ephesians* (Black's NT Commentaries) (London 2001), p. 201.

to develop maturity, thus the 'growing up' of the Christian community needs those who accept the responsibility to care for and nurture the faithful.

Mothers do not provide the sole relationship in which a child grows up, but they, or those who fulfil that role, take on the responsibility to ensure that care happens and for that reason they are pivotal. I would argue that the practice of priesthood, as set out in the ordinal, assumes that priests will be pivotal in taking responsibility for the care necessary for the 'growing up' and 'building up' of the communities entrusted to them. Clearly, there are some difficulties in using this language about growing up and moving to maturity, because any given priest will be working with congregations and communities that include individuals who are more mature both in years and faith than she is. As I explore the metaphor I will look further at these issues. At this point I am simply pointing out the parallels between the maternal demand to create and maintain the relationships and environments in which children themselves can develop towards maturity and the parish priest's role to create and maintain the Christian community of the local church in which and through which people are able to grow ever deeper in faith and understanding. To quote Muddiman on Ephesians 4 again:

> This ecclesiastical use of the metaphor of childhood and parenthood should be kept in mind ... household and Church are closely related ideas.[4]

In both the home and the church, the mother or priest is a facilitator. It is the children and people who themselves do the growing and maturing. Yet there is an important role for the ones who shape and sustain the relationships, spaces and communities in which the growing up happens.

It is because of these parallels in facilitating growth and maturity that the demands Ruddick outlines for maternal practice can provide a way of reflecting on the practice of parish ministry. If we explore her idea of preservation, fostering growth and acceptability, they can easily translate into parish ministry. There is a demand to preserve and protect the faithful, to provide the necessities to sustain their life and to have a ministry of 'holding' and comforting. There is also a demand to foster and nurture growth, to provide an environment in which individuals and communities can explore, grow and mature. This requires a willingness to let people be themselves, to take risks and to embrace change. Alongside these demands is the third, acceptability. Within the context of Christian ministry this is about teaching and maintaining the boundaries of faith. The priest represents the authority of the wider Church; she is to bear witness to the apostolic faith and to teach people the truths of that faith, its virtues and values. There is a requirement to work within the structures of the denomination and wider Christian family with all its complexities. Acceptability for a parish priest also has another dimension, for the priest has a duty to God. Her ministry and the lives of those she cares for and encounters are, the ordinal states, 'to be a living sacrifice acceptable to God'.

---

[4]   Ibid., p. 205.

It follows that, as in mothering, these demands are all good, but may often conflict. This internal conflict between goods is an important point for clergy to grasp. It means that they need to develop the capacity to respond well contingently, and to judge wisely between competing goods. In learning how to lovingly preserve, encourage growth and hold true to the inheritance of faith, a priest has to develop the capacity to think and act as an authentic priest in a myriad of different circumstances, working with unique individuals. She will serve individuals and communities who are constantly changing and who are trying to live out their faith in an unpredictable world. In this chapter we will look further at these demands and the cognitive capacities and virtues that can help clergy in this practice.

Labouring and Action

In the first chapter I noted that it is difficult to define what clergy actually do. If we follow the analogy outlined above, then clergy, like mothers, are engaged in a practice which is often difficult to quantify and articulate. De Marneffe points this out in terms of maternal practice:

> In our society, mothers themselves must create the context in which their mothering takes place; and both structuring the environment and directing the activities within it are indeed hard work. Further, the goals of mothering activity are more open-ended, and the application of skills less quantifiable and more improvisational, than those usually provided by jobs.[5]

Thus she identifies both the difficulties in quantifying maternal work and the way that mothers have to create the context in which their mothering takes place. By this she means more than simply maintaining the home, although that is included, this involves the many tasks and attitudes that shape the spaces and relationships in which a child develops and grows. If clergy are engaged in a kind of spiritual homemaking, in the broadest sense of the term, then this chapter needs to explore how parish clergy create the context in which their *ministry* takes place, structuring the environment and directing the activities within it.

It is interesting at this point to note that clergy and mothers face a similar problem in trying to define what this creation and maintenance of their context consists of. As I said in the first chapter, it is possible to come up with a list of tasks that clergy need to do. These will involve both generic tasks, organising services, presiding at the sacraments and engaging in routine pastoral work, and also tasks specific to that place and community. However, it was clear in the opening chapter that this purely functional account of parish ministry was unsatisfactory. Alongside the tasks of ministry are all the more ephemeral aspects of building up the people

---

[5]   de Marneffe, *Maternal Desire*, p. 114.

of God. It is here that Arendt's categories of human activity – labour, work and action – can provide an insightful framework for understanding the role.

The practice of mothering and the practice of ministry both involve a complex mix of labouring and action with very little work or fabrication. Neither practice is involved with making a product. This is why ideas about work that value blueprints, formulas and measurable targets are unhelpful in assessing maternal or ministerial practice. Accepting that there are not tangible outcomes is an important part of ministry, as is acknowledging that the work is never finished. There will be projects that end and tasks that can be completed, but they all lead on to more projects, more tasks, new things, new needs and a never-ending process of living.

Those engaged in mothering and ministry, in creating the spaces and relationships in which individuals and communities can grow and flourish, need to labour. Arendt defined this as the cyclical repetition of tasks that are involved in the sustaining of life. For mothering this means the daily round of domestic chores: feeding, washing, tidying up and maintaining all the necessities of daily living. Such tasks can be rewarding, but in reality can often feel mundane, tedious and menial. Arendt reminds us that this is the kind of work assigned to servants or even slaves. In her understanding such work was at one level meaningless but it is an important aspect of Christian theology to understand this service as a gift to those we serve. The New Testament offers us a way of appropriating service as a way of loving God and our neighbour. This is possible when the mundane tasks are intricately interwoven with the meaningful concept of action. Service is done for a purpose; to enable the development of the community and the web of relationships with people and God that build up the church.

If we look at the work of parish clergy, then it may appear sacrilegious to refer to the ongoing round of services as labouring and I would not want to suggest that they should equate to drudgery. Yet, even though each event may need careful crafting, they are passing occasions in which people's necessities for being sustained in word and sacrament are met. At some level, as the name implies, these are *services*, organised to serve God and the people, not for their own sake. The spiritual feeding, cleansing and 'tidying' that is provided by the regular services of the Church are the ways in which life is sustained and nourished. They are of course also part of the action, the building up of relationships between people and God, yet they need the labouring service to be done diligently and well. They require practical preparations and the regular maintenance of clean and tidy places. Aspects of ministerial practice therefore involve the menial tasks of domestic labour, from dusting the church to ensuring that there is wine in the sacristy and the linen is clean. It is in this aspect of ministry that clergy are most truly *servants*, providing the sustenance that others need for their lives.

Arendt reminds us that labouring is collective. Clearly these tasks can, and usually are, shared. They can be done collectively, but someone has to know that they will be done. Whoever does them needs to be acknowledged and thanked, for the preservation of life depends on such labouring. It is inappropriate to be dismissive of the maintenance involved in parish ministry, especially when it is implied that it is opposed to the mission of the Church. Maintenance of buildings and the regular work of cleaning, preparing and servicing the church's services are integral to parish ministry. An untidy, dirty and uncared for church speaks to those within and without about a lack of care and a neglect for God's mission.

As I noted above this labouring, servant ministry needs to be understood as intricately connected to Arendt's category of action. For the purpose of ministry is not simply to create tidy places, but to build and sustain networks of relationships and communities in which people can grow and mature in their ability to love God and their neighbour. It is far harder to articulate this activity because it is about the interaction of people and all the possibilities that arise from such relationships. In terms of the Church it goes beyond Arendt's understanding of human interaction, for it is also about the possibilities that arise out of human relationships with God, who in Christ has revealed himself as one who relates. So, aspects of the services of the Church are at the level of labour, in that they sustain life, but at the same time they are the means by which people engage with each other and with the living God. Out of these engagements individuals and communities grow and flourish through the deepening and renewal of the relationships between God and neighbour. For such relationships to flourish we need in ministry as in mothering, the capacity to attend well to the particularity of those we care for.

Particularity and Attention

At the beginning of *The Human Condition* Arendt writes:

> Plurality is the condition of human action because we are all the same, that is, human, in such a way that nobody is ever the same as anyone else who ever lived, lives or will live.[6]

Because relationships are at the heart of *action*, one of the fundamental virtues necessary for the parish priest is attentive love which Ruddick described as both a virtue and a discipline. This attention is necessary for recognising the subjectivity of others and the particularity that arises out of plurality. Such recognition is important in building up and sustaining relationships and communities. Attention, as we saw in the previous chapter, requires the ability to see the real and particular and to eschew the fantasy. This ability is a necessary component of inter-subjective relationships and, particularly, relationships that involve caring. It takes discipline to maintain inter-subjectivity; it is all too easy to objectify the other or project fantasies onto them. Noddings notes how relationships of care, especially when institutionalised, can degenerate into objectivity:

---

[6]   Arendt, *The Human Condition*, p. 8.

To be treated as 'types' instead of individuals, to have strategies exercised on us, objectifies us. We become 'cases' instead of persons. Those of us who are able to escape such situations do so with alacrity, but escape is not always possible. The fact is that many of us have been reduced to cases by the very machinery that has been instituted to care for us.[7]

The virtue and discipline of attentive love needs to be cultivated to avoid the temptation to objectify the other.

This attentiveness in parish ministry is necessary in both ongoing relationships and fleeting encounters. Some relationships involve attending over time, learning the particularities of individuals and communities, building up a knowledge that helps the priest respond appropriately. Such relationships can also involve the priest in learning how to help others articulate and understand unexpressed needs. Yet even sustained relationships need to allow for surprises and new insights, for people change and circumstances are different. In the more fleeting encounters clergy need to quickly attend and ascertain what is required, judging how to respond appropriately. All of this takes discipline and practice as the ability to read and assess people and situations is honed. Many priests do this well, but it is rarely acknowledged as a *discipline* and *skill* that takes time, patience and openness to learn. Clergy need to constantly guard against the temptation to treat people as types, to make lazy assumptions about what they require. On the other hand, they need to guard against being over-intrusive in offering care, which, as we saw in mothering, can stem from a need to see people as needy in order to validate one's own ministry.

In parish ministry clergy are not just attending to people as individuals but also relating to a community and congregation. We saw in Ruddick's work that attention meant an eschewing of fantasy and recognition of reality. This is a particularly important issue for clergy in relating to the congregations and communities they care for. Many clergy find it relatively straightforward to attend well to individuals; an interest in people and a capacity to care are often part of what draws people into the role in the first place. What can be harder is realising how important it is to let go of fantasies about the congregation or the parish. This involves letting go of the fantasy parish, the one in her head, the one the books are about, or the bishop described, or even as the parish profile described! It definitely means acknowledging that even if this looks a bit like a previous parish, it is not the same.

Mothers soon learn that a second child, however similar he may look, has his own character and will need different responses from her. Just as mothers need to learn through trial and error how the actual child differs from the abstract child of the antenatal classes or the ones described in the childcare books, so clergy need to learn through practice about the real parish and people entrusted to their care. This involves taking context seriously and trying to understand the stories that make up this place and this community. Ruddick stresses that mothering involves a valuing

---

[7] Noddings, *Caring*, p. 66.

of concrete ways of thinking, and this is essential in moving from general ideas about how churches and parishes behave to the reality of *this* place and *these* people.

Clearly it is possible and valuable to learn about ways of doing ministry through looking at generalised situations and listening to the experiences and practices of others. There will be many practices that can easily be transposed between different people, places and circumstances. Many things that worked in one place may work well in another. But it must also be acknowledged that many things will not work. Or they need to be explained differently or adjusted appropriately. There are immense overlaps in the way I respond to my two children, but there are also recognisable differences. Strategies that worked with one have never been helpful with the other; the things that delight and stimulate each are in certain ways very different. I have needed to learn through practice what is right for each one.

Clergy can come to a parish with many resources, things they have learned in training, things they have learned through practising ministry elsewhere, but they still need to attend carefully to the particularity of this place and accept that it is a new relationship which will call for some different ways of thinking and acting. The differences may be subtle but the failure to acknowledge them often accounts for tensions and conflict between clergy and their communities. It is no good blaming the people if a particular project that flew in one place fails in the next; instead there needs to be reflection on what is different and why.

We have also noted that this is about inter-subjective relationships, so the reality and actuality of the priest also impacts on the relationship and the way the community develops. I bring to my mothering and my ministry who I am. In attending to the other, the priest needs to adapt to this community, but there also needs to be a developing relationship that enables the community to adapt to the strengths and weaknesses of the priest, who is not going to be the same as the one before. Honesty about oneself can help in managing the expectations of others and make it easier for them to see the real person they are relating to. Recognising that people project their fantasies onto you can be helpful in learning how to challenge unrealistic expectations and the temptation to collude. Clearly, not all conflict is a result of failure to attend. However, disappointed expectations for clergy and their congregations result from a failure to eschew fantasy and attend to the particularity and context. Such mistaken expectations can lead to unnecessary conflict.

There is no such thing as an abstract church. Nicholas Healy in *Church, World and the Christian Life* describes how 'blueprint ecclesiology' arising from abstract thinking can play a necessary part in thinking and writing about the Church in general. However, he argues that the concrete context of the real Church must be acknowledged in discussions of eccelsiology. Any models put forward as abstract are in fact shaped by an imaginative understanding of Church, which is often unacknowledged. Therefore any 'blueprint' ecclesiology needs to be treated with care. If such models do not allow for concrete contextual adjustments, he claims, there can be a misjudgement of the focus of ministry when the blueprint is used to shape the ministry in a real place:

A given blueprint ecclesiology may indeed respond adequately to its context. But, again, the lack of such analysis increases the likelihood that it will not, even though it may be consonant with Scripture and tradition. In such a case the theologian would have misconstrued the historical movement of the Church and its present shape, or misinterpreted the ecclesiological context or both. As a result the blueprint, although fine as a presentation of doctrine, would be unfruitful or impractical in the concrete in that like most bad judgements, it would respond to what is peripheral rather than to what is central. And because the blueprint is developed without explicit consideration of the ecclesiological context, it may well take longer to recognise its inadequacy.[8]

This is important when assessing the kinds of initiatives around mission and church growth that often fail to acknowledge the real complexity of contextual ministry. Healy uses the terminology of blueprints and it is interesting to note how this relates to Arendt's work category, which, I argued, is not principally applicable to parish ministry. Although the importance of contextual ministry is increasingly emphasised, initiatives from diocesan offices or courses on Church leadership can imply that *there are* formulas, blueprints and measurable outcomes that fit all churches.[9] Just as all people are unique, so are all parishes and congregations. There may be many similarities, but no two places are the same and no parish stays the same because they are made up of people.

To attend properly to the particularity of a parish means time spent in what might look like 'doing nothing'. Stadlen suggests that this is how observers perceive a mother's need to spend time simply sitting and looking at her child; it appears as if she is doing nothing but in fact she is looking, listening and learning. Just so, parish clergy need to look, listen and absorb the community they are called to serve. It means listening to the stories of people and watching how they interact. It means in practical terms time spent visiting, drinking coffee, reading old accounts of the parish and local history. It means learning the geography of the place, seeing where people spend their time and spending time with them. It means finding out what they are proud of, what delights them and what disappoints or shames them. It takes time and is ongoing.

Clergy who spend a long time in a place may know it well but they, too, have to attend to the changes, shifts in demographics and local self-understanding. Good clergy do this attending, often without consciously setting out to. Their interest in people and their stories means that they are keen to listen and to understand

---

[8]   Nicholas Healey, *Church, World and the Christian Life* (Cambridge 2000), p. 47.

[9]   The Church of England's General Synod discussed Mission Action Plans at its July 2011 meeting and whether to have a national Mission Action Plan. These do include an assessment of context, but have a tendency to become formulaic and driven by only one aspect of parish life: that of numerical growth. There is an assumption that a five-year action plan can fix the parishes' priorities, which seems to leave little room for contingent circumstances.

the particularity of a place. In arriving to work in a new church, clergy need to learn that it is not always the people who are most ready to tell you 'how it is' who have the most accurate vision. It involves putting together a picture from a multiplicity of images and accounts, many of which will be biased and some positively skewed. As the priest attends to the community's own stories, she can begin to help interpret their account of the church and the parish. Yet the story is ongoing and changing, so time spent attending to the concrete reality of a community is always a central aspect of ministry. It may look like *doing nothing* but it is in chatting and listening to others, being involved in the local community and catching up on the gossip that communities are understood and relationships created and maintained.

Loving Attention and Asymmetric Relationships

Ruddick links attention to love. It is not simply to recognise the other's subjectivity, but to look at them lovingly with compassion and a willingness to care. It seems much easier to understand loving attention in the context of a mother and child than it does in the complex relationships of a parish priest. Noddings, in expounding an ethics of care, notes that in some caring relationships it is relatively easy to care – it feels 'natural'. This, she would say, is usually true of maternal caring, yet there is, she claims, an ethical caring, when we have to deliberately choose to care for another whom we don't easily love by making ourselves think about how we would respond to them if we did love them. This is done by drawing on previous experiences of caring and of being cared for, but also through a deliberate discipline.[10]

Through ordination clergy have made a commitment to care. In accepting the responsibility of a given parish they have made a commitment to care for this place and these people. 'Receive the cure of souls which is yours and mine', the bishop says. In order to attend lovingly to these people clergy need to utilise the capacity for ethical caring, but they do so using theological resources. At the heart of the Christian faith is the belief that each person we encounter is already loved by God and is made in the image of God. Although it is still necessary for a priest to draw on her own experience of past caring encounters, there is this added theological dimension to help her care. These people are beloved of God who Himself loves and cares for her. Noddings would firmly reject this theological ethic, but for clergy it is a central motivational factor in attending to the other. To recognise that the other, however difficult we may find them, is precious in God's sight does not blind us to their faults; instead we are told to recognise the Christ in their needs and in loving Him we can love and serve our neighbours. This involves a cognitive capacity and a virtue, the capacity to think theologically

---

[10]   Noddings, *Starting at Home*, p. 30.

about the worth of each person and acknowledge their kinship and the virtue of love, particularly love of neighbour.

There is, of course, a danger in this theological position. It might work against recognising the subjectivity of the other and could lead clergy into seeing people and situations as types. This temptation to slip out of inter-subjective relationships into ones that, however benign the intention, objectify others is made more likely by the asymmetrical nature of many of the encounters clergy engage in. Although the actual status of clergy may be ambiguous, the reality is that once ordained, people relate to them as having authority. As they engage in the activity of parish ministry clergy find themselves in asymmetrical relationships of caring, of teaching, of leading and ministering. That is not to say that *all* relationships within the parish will be asymmetrical. Clergy will have many different relationships of friendship, collegiality and individuals who provide *them* with care and nurture, but the role means that they have responsibilities that place them consistently in a position where others are, albeit transitionally, dependent on them for a variety of reasons.

Asymmetric relationships are valuable because they provide this luxury of transitional dependence. That is, they are the kind of relationships in which, for a period, we can rely on the other for something that we need. The mother/child relationship needs to be asymmetrical because the child is in need of care and protection. It is asymmetrical for a long time, but the aim is that the child gradually does grow and the levels of dependency shift and change. However, it is not just children who need the luxury of transitional dependence; there are many encounters that we have as adults where the relationship works because, at some level, one is caring and the other cared for. Noddings talks about such relationships being 'generously unequal'. She discusses this in her role as a teacher:

> Occasional equal meetings may occur between teacher and student, of course, but the meetings between teacher as teacher and student as student are necessarily and generously unequal.[11]

That is, the student does not have a responsibility for the teacher of the same kind that the teacher has for the student. The teacher's role is to free the student by the way that she cares for him; there is no expectation of the student reciprocating in kind.

At one level such relationships are clearly unequal, but where they are motivated by the desire to free the other and to enable them to flourish, the inequality is in role, not in substance, as Alistair McFadyen in *The Call to Personhood* points out:

> In dialogue, equality refers to a formal identity between the partners, to the quality of their intersubjective engagement. It does not refer to their material identities, or to an equality in the quantity of the social space-time they occupy ... A purely quantitative notion of equality issues in a tit-for-tat understanding of personal

---

[11]   Noddings, *Caring*, p. 67.

relationships where every communication has to receive a response equal in
quantity, where every gift has to be returned.[12]

Thus it follows that asymmetric relationships, especially when shaped by role,
can be inter-subjective. Where the role requires an asymmetry in the relationship,
there is a particular responsibility on the part of the one who has the power, who
is able to do something, to focus on the subjectivity of the other. This involves
recognising them as a unique individual in a unique set of circumstances, however
similar they may be to other people or other situations.

The vast majority of relationships formed during parish ministry will be at
some level asymmetric, in which the priest has a responsibility to care, because
she is the priest. Many encounters are intended as relationships of pastoral care
in which the priest is expected to attend carefully to the other. However, in *all*
relationships and encounters with people the priest is aware that she is available to
be used in this way and that her role requires her to respond with care if necessary.
This does not mean that she has to do everything or meet every need herself, but
it does mean that she has to practise the discipline of attending well. This is the
reality of the relationship and the responsibility of ordination.

One of the complexities for parish clergy is that most of their encounters do
not have clear boundaries. The asymmetric relationships of teachers to students,
doctors to patients or counsellors to their clients are usually carried out in specific
places and times, but parish clergy, like mothers, live within the context of their
work. Stadlen comments that for mothers this means they learn to be 'instantly
interruptible'.[13] In making this statement she is acknowledging that one of the
most overwhelming aspects for new parents is that they are not in control of
the times they are needed by the child. This is not the same as being constantly
engaged with the child, though sometimes it can feel like it! There will be times
when the child sleeps and, later, time when he plays on his own and, still later, long
periods when he is responsible for himself and there is little the mother actually
has to do for him. However, a vital aspect of the relationship is that sense of being
expected to switch on full attention when needed. Sometimes the signals are clear
– the child demands attention – but at other times it needs a careful reading of the
particular child and their circumstances to know that some response is needed.
This interruptibility and the need to suddenly switch into an attentive responsive
role is a recognisable aspect of parish ministry.

Clergy may have more boundaries than mothers, but they also have far more
people to attend to. The reality of the relationship means they find themselves

---

[12]   Alistair McFadyen, *The Call to Personhood* (Cambridge 1990), pp. 144–5. Like
Noddings, McFadyen looks at how different professional relationships demand asymmetry
in order to work. He uses the example of a consultant doctor: 'The social space-time
appropriate to each is quite properly bounded by the professional relationship orientated
towards the health needs of the patient.'

[13]   Stadlen, *What Mothers Do*, ch. 4.

expected to focus on the needs of the other in unplanned and unexpected circumstances. They can feel constantly interrupted. Some encounters are, of course, planned and organised, but the way in which clergy live and work amongst their parishioners means that they need to develop the ability to notice when a conversation moves from general small talk to something specific that needs attending to. They need to learn to look and listen and notice. This doesn't mean that they indiscriminately drop everything for anyone who wants to talk. There needs to be prioritising and sometimes, with both adults and children, suggestions can be made about appropriate times to talk further or explore an issue more deeply or to take issues somewhere else. What it does mean for both mothers and priests is that the moments that require deep attention to the other are not easily scheduled and happen in the midst of the mundane and ordinary. When these moments happen they require what Noddings calls 'motivational displacement'; a willingness to put aside one's own focus for a limited timespan so that the other becomes the centre of attention.

It is important to note the limited timespan of such motivational displacement. The 'putting aside' of one's own needs is a necessary but time-limited aspect of attending to the other. It is not a constant process of self negation. Inter-subjective relationships need two subjects. Clergy need to find a sense of their own subjectivity both in and beyond the practice of their ministry. To be available for others does not necessitate losing sight of one's own needs and concerns. It is important, therefore, that there are ongoing and momentary relationships in which the priest is cared for herself and where she can rest on the generosity of others. Through such experiences her own sense of being valued needs to be maintained.

Central to her ministry is prayer and worship, those experiences in which she is able to refresh her sense of being cared for and dependent on God. The value of saying the offices means points in each day when the burden of care can be given in prayer to God and the priest can know herself to be held in God's loving arms. This reminder of who she is and how she is cared for by God can help to prevent a lack of subjectivity on the part of the priest. This matters because a loss of subjectivity, a move into self-denial can lead to over-intrusive caring; the need to be needed. Ruddick describes the temptation of mothers to equate self-denial with love. She sees this as a particular temptation because mothers have been encouraged to see self-sacrifice as a good thing. They have been encouraged to see denying their own needs for the sake of their children's as laudable. Yet this denial of their own needs has often involved a projection of their own needs onto their children in a kind of over-intrusive caring. Again she uses theological language concluding that:

> The soul that can empty itself is a soul that already has a known, respected, albeit ever-developing self to return to when the moment of attention has passed.[14]

---

[14] Ibid., p. 122.

What Ruddick writes here about mothers is also true for parish priests. They bring to their work a whole language about servanthood and self-sacrifice. This can mean that clergy are often tempted to 'court self-denial', equating this with *agape* and Christian service. They may then project their need to be needed onto the people they serve as those cared for become necessary for validating the sense of sacrifice. It is this kind of perverted attention that unwittingly seeks to keep people dependent. It can easily lead to manipulative behaviour and sometimes a deep resentment towards those who are being served.[15]

It is important in ministry, therefore, to acknowledge the difference between the time-limited experiences of self-renunciation that attentive love calls for and the self-abnegation that is one of its degenerate forms. To be there for another *is* time-limited even if in some relationships, like mothering, the timespan is great. This shift of focus away from the self and onto the other is set in a concrete situation that exists in a particular time. Different levels of need and vulnerability will dictate how long one needs to attend to the other. However, what Noddings describes as 'a motivational displacement' is not the same as an ongoing attitude of self-denial and self-sacrifice unconnected to specific people and situations. To court sacrifice for its own sake is not a Gospel imperative, while to be prepared to lay down one's life for a friend is. Christians are all called to love our neighbours and to be focused on the ways in which we can help others, and for some this may mean living lives of heroic self-giving and even acts of martyrdom. What is essential is the relational aspect of such acts and the concrete reality which calls for them. Caring, times of self-sacrifice and being at the disposal of the other are all called for and motivated by the *actual* needs of a *genuine* other, not a projection of one's own need to be needed or a false belief that all sacrifice is somehow Christ-like.[16]

Thus it follows that clergy need to be ready to attend, ready to care but also confident in their own subjectivity. This is important because the ability to attend to others' needs requires the capacity to see things from a wider perspective. Clergy need to be able to both feel for the other but also offer a reflective response to them. This involves recognising and attending to feelings that are different from one's own but are real and valid to those caught up in them. Many pastoral encounters will involve people facing situations that are outside the priest's personal experience and people will react and respond to such circumstances in different ways. In attending to people and communities the ability to both

---

[15] An insightful article on this tendency for self-sacrifice to degenerate into manipulative behaviour is written by Brita Gill-Austern, 'Love Understood as Self-Sacrifice and Self-Denial: What Does it Do to Women?', in J. Stevenson Moessner (ed.), *Through the Eyes of Women* (Minneapolis 1996), pp. 304–21.

[16] The essay by Beverly Wildung Harrison, 'The Power of Anger in the Work of Love', in C.S. Robb (ed.), *Making the Connections* (Boston 1985), pp. 3–21, esp. p. 19, which explores the way sacrifice and crucifixion become confused with imagery of love.

sympathise in the true sense of the word and yet offer perspective means that the priest needs to have a dual focus:

> When I attend in this way I become, in an important sense, a duality. I see through two pairs of eyes, hear with two sets of ears, feel the pain of the other self in addition to my own.[17]

So writes Noddings. In saying this she is affirming the one-caring's ability to genuinely recognise and sympathise with the reality of the other's needs while still being able to see things from outside the situation. This involves the capacity to reflect on and articulate emotions and feelings. It is this ability to both recognise and value the feelings of others but not be overwhelmed by the other's emotions that is useful in being able to comfort and support them.

Recent studies looking at attachment in mothers and children has some interesting light to shed on the mother's sense of self. De Marneffe comments on the findings of interviews with parents about their own childhood experiences:

> What appears decisive is not, as one might expect, the actual attachment experiences parents had with their own caregivers. Rather, it is how parents are able *to think and talk about* these experiences – in other words, their ability to reflect on and communicate about their experiences – that relates to the security of their child. This says something quite striking about the importance not simply of a mother's custodial care, but also her subjectivity … If a mother can reflect, she can more accurately perceive and understand her own and others' thoughts and feelings. This in turn, makes her more likely to be able to respond sensitively to her child.[18]

Thus it follows that a sense of self and the ability to care for others requires reflective thinking that takes feelings seriously. It involves being able to reflect on concrete situations in one's own and others' lives and use the wisdom learned to respond appropriately in new situations. Such reflection also alters the way that failure is understood. Bad experiences, failures in love and care, mistakes and missed opportunities can potentially become, through reflection, opportunities for wisdom. This way of thinking acknowledges that sometimes we only learn to get things right through having experienced times when we or others have got things wrong. By this I am not condoning deliberate wrongdoing, but acknowledging the inadequacies of human response that mean we fail each other.

It is through this ability to learn from one's own and others' experiences by careful reflection that a priest builds up the wisdom and *phronesis* necessary for good practice. She learns not to be overwhelmed by the other's feelings, so caught up in them that she cannot respond, while continuing to be compassionate.

---

[17]   Noddings, *Starting at Home*, p. 14.

[18]   de Marneffe, *Maternal Desire*, pp. 77–8.

Attending leads to a response that may be practical, or it may simply be the ability to acknowledge the reality of the other's feelings and assuring them that someone is there, for however short a time, being with them. This involves that generous inequality possible through the asymmetry of the relationship. Those being cared for know that there is no expectation that they need to shift their focus onto the one-caring.

In parish ministry all those who are seeking God through the rituals of the Church are dependent at some level on the priest to provide for them and nurture them. Clergy, therefore, need to resist any temptations to be manipulative or capricious in the access they provide to the sacraments, worship and ministry of the Church. Pastoral ministry will provide the most intense cases of temporary asymmetric relationships shaped by need. Such encounters need specific relationships of dependence when people are vulnerable and look for care from the clergy. These relationships can take up time and energy, but they can also be affirming and exhilarating. To feel needed is a powerful experience and in a job where it can often be hard to measure the fruitfulness of one's efforts, the instant gratification of intense pastoral relations can be validating. There is, however, a danger if the priest has a low sense of her own subjectivity; she may want to prolong such experiences to increase the affirmation of her role. In attending to the other the priest needs to be able to read the signs that require her to begin to let go before the other feels a sense of obligation or begins to feel smothered.

Whereas in mothering the losses in intimacy are at best replaced by new depths to the ongoing relationship, in ministry these intense pastoral encounters may not lead to rich ongoing relationships. In fact, in some situations where an individual has been particularly vulnerable and needy for a period of time, they may well seek to distance themselves from the priest, who reminds them of this difficult episode in their life. Thus clergy can find themselves deeply needed for a period and then distanced. This can mean that the losses of dependency for clergy may feel similar to rejection. A household suffering a devastating bereavement may for a short time see the priest as a central part of life, a welcome visitor who brings comfort and practical advice into a chaotic and frightening place, but the time will come when that need is over and clergy need to know how to withdraw gracefully allowing normal patterns of relationships to be established. These relationships require the luxury of asymmetry, what Noddings calls 'generous inequality'. People are looking for someone to care for them without expecting to take any responsibility for the carer's needs.

It therefore follows that parish priests need to know how to name and manage the feelings that surround periods of intense transitional dependence. A priest needs to have her own ongoing relationships of interdependence and safe places where she can be sustained. Such relationships can allow her to acknowledge the adrenalin present in intense pastoral experiences and how good it can feel to be needed and, subsequently, how difficult it can be to let go. Other caring professions tend to have clearer boundaries and more robust systems of managing such relationships and feelings. The fluidity of boundaries for clergy with those who are part of the community, and probably the congregation, can make letting go and renegotiating the relationship harder. There are no clear rules about how this is done, and wisdom, experience and self-reflection are necessary to develop care that is neither disinterested nor over-intrusive. Again we see that it is about resisting the temptation to degenerate forms of love and care out of self-protection or self-validation. To be needed and to provide care for those in need is a fulfilling and enriching aspect of human relationships, but it must always be remembered that dependence is transitional and the aim of good ministry is to enable people to develop maturity.

Parish clergy at any one time will be juggling a mixture of intense pastoral relationships that vary in timespan and depth of need, alongside the ongoing relationships required to make and sustain a community. Within the congregation they care for there will be people of different ages, those who have been Christians for differing lengths of time, those who have far wider experiences than them and are confident and self-assured, as well as those who are continuing to feel vulnerable and insecure. The ability to attend well to all these people requires recognising their very different needs and assessing an appropriate response. This requires the virtue of humility; recognising that a priest's role is not to be the focus, but to provide the places and spaces where people can have their needs met by God. Dependence on other human beings is at times appropriate but recognising that our dependency on God is ongoing is a central aspect of the Christian faith. Many of those who come to church simply require the priest to facilitate the kind of worship experience that enables them to renew and affirm their dependence on God. They want to receive the grace necessary for them to continue to develop as Christians in the world and they are not looking for a lot of hands-on care.

Bruce Reed in *The Dynamics of Worship*[19] maintains that good worship provides a ritualised experience of the way humans oscillate between the need for dependence and independence and how this needs to be focused on our overall dependence on God.[20] The sacraments and rituals of the Church should provide an external experience of being dependent on God and blessed by God, sending individuals and communities back out into their world with a stronger internal faith. In a sense, the priest's role in this is not to get in the way, but to enable the worship of the Church, the reality of the sacraments, the preaching of the word and the strength of the fellowship to regularly feed and reassure, challenge and re-order people's internal faith and practice.

---

[19]　Bruce Reed was the founder of the Grubb Institute of Behavioural Studies, which encourages the use of systemic thinking to look at how communities and organisations work. In *The Dynamics of Worship* (London 1978), Reed sets out his oscillation theory of worship in which he sees the Eucharist as an event that enables worshippers to move into a dynamic experience of their dependence on God in order to be able to re-internalise that dependence as they are sent out into the world to confront its complexities.

[20]　Ibid., pp. 13–14.

This does involve the priest in making sure that the diet provided in church is varied enough and rich enough for the breadth of experience of the congregation. As the worship experience is part of maintaining the sense of attachment to God, it also needs to offer the kind of familiarity that enables people to comfortably rest on God. A priest needs to attend to the needs of the long-time worshipper and the newcomers, practising a hospitality that draws people in while not being over-intrusive into the worshipping lives of those who know what they are doing. She needs to recognise that changes in worship can be unsettling to those who have found certain practices helpful and yet, sometimes, new ways of doing things and new ideas may provide people with stimulus to deepen their faith and understanding. Her role also means having the humility to listen to and learn from the older and wiser Christians within her congregation. It is important not to patronise those who, outside the church, deal with complex issues and weighty responsibilities. Thus, in preaching and teaching, the kinds of questions and issues that impact on the real lives of those who come need to be addressed, enabling them to find their concerns connected to the ongoing story of Christian faith.

Thus the relationship of clergy to their congregation has parallels with the kind of relationships between mothers and adolescents or adult children. There is a stage in life where a child is independent in many areas where he used to be dependent. My teenage children want a fully stocked fridge with the right sort of food, clean washing and frequent lifts. I can be a good mother simply by getting this right and staying out of the way! When I am tired or unwell they will make me cups of tea, take some interest in my concerns and show some care. They also engage in interesting conversations that can stretch and challenge me, share in common interests and provide adult company. They are on the way to maturity. However, something in their life may trigger a greater need of me and the almost-adult needs for a while to be a child again.

A good parish priest will have a multiplicity of rich, interdependent relationships within the church they serve. For some what is necessary is that the worship is well prepared and the spiritual food regularly and generously provided. Others will want the stimulation of talking, arguing, sharing and enjoying time together in relationships of equality while some will generously attend to the priest's well-being. Yet she is always their priest, so when life circumstances unsettle or undermine, then she needs to be ready to offer the dependency they need for as long as *they* need it.

To summarise this chapter, I have been arguing that parish ministry, like mothering, involves a relationship centred in particularity. Clergy accept the responsibility to care for a particular set of people in a given place. This means that they need to value concrete thinking and the ability to attend to the other. They are called into relationships which, for periods of time, are asymmetrical and it is important that such relationships remain inter-subjective. This means a proper recognition of the other and the ability, for a necessary timespan, to focus on the reality of who they are and what they need. This does not require an ongoing attitude of self-denial, but needs careful maintenance of the priest's own sense of being a loved self. The ability to respond well appropriately, to attend lovingly to the other and to value concrete thinking are all aspects of ministerial practice. Teaching, training and preparation can help affirm the importance of these aspects of ministry but they are learned and honed through practice and the ability to reflect on practice. And, as Ruddick reminds us, to name them is not to possess them, but to point to both the temptations to be guarded against and the good practice to be aimed for.

Chapter 8
The Virtue of Humility
and the Issue of Power

Parish clergy are placed in positions which have authority and power, but power is a difficult concept for clergy to talk about. There is an ambiguity about power in terms of parish relationships and as we noted in the first chapter authority is circumspect and contested. Power is also an ambiguous term for mothers. It can be hard for them to acknowledge the power they have over dependent and vulnerable children and this very power can, at times, be so overwhelming that, in fact, they feel powerless. This sense of powerlessness is compounded by their social status and the many 'experts' who seem to know how they should be doing things better. And, above all, discussions of power and control can seem out of place in a relationship that is meant to consist of love.

It is for similar reasons that clergy find the concept of their power difficult. They, too, feel a complex mixture of powerlessness in the face of a role that is never complete, carried out within a context where many 'experts' seem to hold up impossible expectations. They also need to understand the place of power in a practice that is meant to be shaped by service and love. And yet, if they are honest, they can acknowledge that they have great power in people's lives. They act as gatekeepers to the sacraments and rituals of the Church, they speak in the name of God with the power to forgive and to bless and through their teaching, preaching and leading of the congregational worship they shape people's attitudes to God, to themselves and to others. As parish priests they have authority within the Church and the community even though this authority is circumspect. They have a responsibility to care for these people. This chapter will look at how that responsibility shapes attitudes to the power a priest has and the virtues that are necessary for collaborative patterns of ministry.

As I noted in the last chapter, humility is a central virtue for priests in managing the asymmetric relationships of care and the collaborative relationships that are characteristic of parish ministry. In maternal practice humility was identified as the virtue needed to guard against the temptation of intrusive, over-protective mothering or neglectful and ineffectual care; these are, I suggest, particular manifestations of distorted power – domination and passivity – that have strong parallels in parish ministry. Ruddick explores humility within the context of a mother's fantasy that perfect control is possible; that she can do everything to keep her child safe. She suggests that mothers must learn that the world is complex and much is beyond their control.[1]

---

[1]   Ruddick, *Maternal Thinking*, p. 72.

She defends her use of the word 'control' in the context of caring for children, but in the context of parish ministry I will use the term 'responsibility'. So, to paraphrase Ruddick, a parish priest without humility may become frantic in her efforts to be responsible for everything but she cannot, out of degenerate humility or passivity, relinquish the responsibility that comes with her charge. And for a priest humility not only means acknowledging the unpredictability of chance and individual people, but also the inability of knowing the overarching plans of God. Humility, therefore, is about having a proper understanding of what falls within an individual's capacity to act and is therefore connected to ideas of power. A proper understanding of what falls within one's control guards against dominating patterns of leadership, where the priest knows all the answers. It also guards against a passive inability to exercise authority appropriately.

To explore this idea further it is important to acknowledge that the asymmetric nature of many clergy encounters and relationships make misuse of power a stronger temptation. Arendt maintains that in the realm of action, the web of human relating, power is always present, but it is not necessarily negative. She draws a contrast between power and force:

> Power is what keeps the public realm, the potential space of appearance between acting and speaking men in existence ... if it could be possessed like strength or applied like force instead of being dependent upon the unreliable and only temporary agreement of many wills and intentions, omnipotence would be a concrete human possibility.[2]

For Arendt force belongs in the realm of work. It is appropriate in the making of products, but not in human action.

Parish ministry has little to do with achieving tangible ends. This is important in trying to understand how power in ministry must be utilised collaboratively; it must not be understood as strength or force. Where modes of assessing success that more readily fit Arendt's concept of work, such as blueprints, measurable targets and quantifiable results, are inappropriately imported into the realm of action then wrong attitudes to collaboration may result. If the programme is being driven by clearly definable ends then it makes sense for a more directional less consensual style of leadership. If a priest sees her role in leading the parish as implementing a fixed plan, rather than the uncertainty of continually developing a collaborative vision, then, whatever her intentions she will be tempted to lead by strength or, at the worst, a form of force. A battle of wills may then follow.

Arendt's understanding of power offers an important corrective to misconceptions; she notes that power 'can be divided without decreasing it':

> For power, like action, is boundless ... Its only limitation is the existence of other people, but this limitation is not accidental, because human power corresponds

---

[2]   Arendt, *The Human Condition*, p. 200.

to the condition of plurality to begin with. For the same reason, power can be divided without decreasing it, and the interplay of powers with their checks and balances is even liable to generate more power, so long, at least, as the interplay is alive and has not resulted in a stalemate.[3]

This reminds us that power is not a finite quantity that needs to be wrested from each other. Instead in human relationships power has the capacity to be shared and to be generative. Where the virtue of humility is cultivated there is a right understanding of power, which should enable collaborative relationships to flourish.

In parish ministry good practice must include generative power-sharing. The Church of England has developed structures for this; elected officers, PCCs and various deanery and diocesan bodies are meant to share power generatively to build up the whole Church. Alongside these formal structures are the informal networks of relationships within any parish – with complex power dynamics. The parish priest has particular responsibilities within all these structures. As I said in the first chapter, the current understanding of parish ministry is of collaborative decision-making and strategising. In order to do this, priests need to understand the difference between delegation and collaboration. They need to understand the difference between learning how to negotiate vision and imposing a plan. They also need to acknowledge the shared nature of parish ministry and the way power can be shared without being diminished.

The importance of collaborative patterns of ministry is central to Pickard's work, which we looked at in the first chapter. Like Arendt, he sees the power that arises from human interaction as potentially generative:

> Life in relation to others involves the exercise of power. Contrary to popular rhetoric these days power per se is not a bad thing, nor is it a necessary evil ... A collaborative approach to ministry requires both sharing of power and a generous bestowal of power. This is a deeply regenerative action and increases the power available. However, this dynamic is counter-intuitive and something most of us resist out of fear of our own diminution.[4]

He identifies the degenerative failures in collaborative ministry as 'either autocratic or unhealthy submissive forms of relation'.[5] These degenerative ways of relating connect to the ideas of domination and passivity discussed in mothering; the fantasy of perfect control or the despair that leads to abnegating responsibility. He writes:

> The autocratic way in ministry deals with fear and anxiety about loss of control by the exercise of power over others. Power may be released and authority

---

[3] Ibid., p. 201.

[4] Pickard, *Theological Foundations for Collaborative Ministry*, p. 2.

[5] Ibid.

delegated, but this is more often not true delegation but task assignment ... The autocratic leader uses the gifts of others but creativity, where it is allowed, is carefully managed.[6]

Thus the desire to hold on to control, most likely a fantasy of perfect control, leads to a kind of over-management of others. The autocrat tends to replace genuine power with strength or force. I would suggest that the temptation to this autocratic, isolated managerial style is more likely when there is external pressure on clergy to work towards action plans, tick lists and measurable targets.

In contrast to the autocratic or dominant way Pickard describes the temptation in the other direction which leads to a passivity that is unable or unwilling to take appropriate responsibility:

The alternative to autocratic leadership is often an unhealthy submissiveness in which a person's gifts and creativity for ministry are continually suppressed; the voice is lost, vision wanes, stasis sets in, energy levels diminish, creativity dies. In this scenario collaboration is thwarted due to lack of confidence that a person has anything to contribute to shared life and ministry.[7]

In this scenario the leader has lost her sense of her own subjectivity and is therefore allowing others to dominate her. It is an inability to take seriously the responsibility that comes with the role and therefore equates to a form of neglect and a failure to care. He goes on to say:

Both of these defaults feed off isolationist and individual approaches to ministry. There is little or no understanding of what it means to be members 'one to another' (Romans 12:5) orientated towards the other as the ontological foundation of life and ministry.[8]

It follows, therefore, that in ministry, as in motherhood, the responsibilities inherent in the relationship can lead to the temptation to domination or passivity. It is also true in both practices that these degenerative forms of relating can often arise out of genuine desire to do one's best. Domination in mothering can be motivated by the desire to protect the child, to help her fit in socially, to minimise risk and pain. The tendency to passivity may come from a belief that others know better what is right for the child or that the child's independent freedom makes boundaries inappropriate. Similarly in parish ministry, autocratic styles of leadership may be motivated by a sincere belief that the priest knows what is best to preserve the life and faith of the people, that her role and training means she has a duty to impose a particular vision. This may be shaped by an adherence to

---

[6] Ibid.

[7] Ibid., p. 3.

[8] Ibid.

a strict tradition so that conformity is valued over exploration. Also priests may believe that their understanding of God or their theology of priesthood demands an autocratic style of leadership. Where theology prizes conformity to a narrowly defined understanding of a proper Christian, it is easy to see how ministerial work falls more easily into the realm of 'work'. The aim, in that case, is to produce a recognisable finished article of a good Christian; the danger is that people become commodities.

On the other hand, priests may move into unhealthy, submissive patterns of ministry because they believe that this is what it means to be a servant. Or they may not trust their own judgements or vision. A genuine liberalism may make them fear imposing boundaries that limit people's freedoms or challenge wrong behaviour. This can also arise out of a fear of conflict and a misguided belief that love is never angry. As Pickard suggests, this passivity can lead to lack of clarity and vision or to circumstances where others in the community become domineering, asserting their own agendas. Clearly there are also practitioners, in both mothering and ministry, who dominate because they have learned that such behaviour makes their life easier or at some level they feel validated by having power over others. And there are those who move to passivity for an easier life, allowing others to fill the vacuum and make the difficult decisions. It is also true that even the best of mothers or clergy manifest aspects of domination or passivity in certain situations. Tiredness, overwork and lack of affirmation can all lead to failures in collaboration and a move to impose one's will or simply give in on a particular issue. Ruddick suggests that humility is a key virtue in guarding against the temptations to domination or passivity in mothering, and I suggest it is also a key virtue to guard against the similar temptations of ministry. As perhaps is the need to get adequate rest and sleep!

To name a virtue is not to possess it but to be aware of the aims of good practice and the temptations to be guarded against. For priests to practise humility does not, of course, guarantee that others will also practise the virtue, but if a priest models a characteristically humble way of relating, it is more likely that others may see the benefits. In the responsibilities of helping others to mature, priests themselves need to practise and model the virtues. Humility, therefore, is about a realistic acceptance of who one is and what one is called to do. It involves acknowledging the power that is intrinsic to the relationship and using it in ways that generate life and growth.

If we turn to one of the Pauline passages about ministry, we find that before the list of ministries in the Church, there is an exhortation to have a realistic sense of self:

> Do not be conformed to this world, but be transformed by the renewing of your minds, so that you may discern what is the will of God – what is good and acceptable and perfect. For by the grace given to me I say to everyone among you not to think of yourself more highly than you ought to think, but to think with sober judgment, each according to the measure of faith that God has assigned.

> For as in one body we have many members, and not all the members have the
> same function, so we, who are many, are one body in Christ, and individually we
> are members one of another.[9]

Christians are called 'not to think of yourself more highly' but to have a 'sober judgement' that acknowledges one's own sense of faith and responsibility within the diversity of gifts. This right sense of subjectivity is connected to the virtue of humility. It precedes Paul's use of the body image, a metaphor for interdependency in building up the life of the Church. Thus, having a right sense of self and being properly humble is necessary if we are to be a community in which we are 'members one of another'. This brings us back to the importance of maintaining inter-subjective relationships that require respect for the reality and particularity of others while guarding against the temptation to dominate. These relationships also require a sense of one's own worth and subjectivity and recognition of one's own gifts and calling, in order to resist the temptation to loss of voice and degeneration into passivity.

Forgiveness and Trust

In *Maternal Thinking* Ruddick connects the virtue of humility to that of cheerfulness. This virtue is necessary to guard against the temptations of cheery denial on the one hand or despair on the other. It needs to be clear-sighted and resilient allowing us 'to start over and over again'.[10] I suggested before that this cheerfulness correlates to the Christian virtue of hope the capacity to continue to believe in new and good possibilities and for Christians to believe that in God all will, in the end, be well. This willingness to start over is generative, connected to birthing imagery; Arendt calls it 'natality' and herself connects it to hope, though without a concept of the divine. Although, neither Ruddick nor Arendt write from a Christian perspective, their concepts of resilient cheerfulness and natality acknowledge that hope is held within the midst of human fallibility and this requires the capacity to forgive and be forgiven.

Arendt notes that action, human relating, has to deal with 'the predicament of irreversibility – of being unable to undo what one has done' and 'unpredictability ... the chaotic uncertainty of the future'.[11] That is, human relationships and communities need to be able to cope with the mistakes, failures and trespasses of human fallibility while maintaining the hope that working together will be fruitful and generative. Forgiveness, she maintains, is necessary for the miscommunications and offences that are made, often unknowingly or unintentionally, through lack of attention as we misread others and trespass

---

[9]   Romans 12:2–5, NRSV.

[10]   Ruddick *Maternal Thinking*, p. 74.

[11]   Arendt, *The Human Condition*, p. 237.

against them. She looks to the teachings of Jesus on forgiveness, while distancing herself from Christianity, seeing his understanding of forgiveness as the clearest philosophical teaching on the subject. She distinguishes between crime and willed evil on the one hand and trespassing on the other. The former, she says, 'according to Jesus ... will be taken care of by God in the last judgement':

> But trespassing is an everyday occurrence which is in the very nature of action's constant establishment of new relationships within a web of relations, and it needs forgiving, dismissing, in order to make it possible for life to go on constantly releasing men from what they have done unknowingly.[12]

It follows that in any generative relationships in the home, church or wider community forgiveness is a necessary component. It allows relationships to flourish despite the inevitable ways in which we from time to time fail to recognise and respond appropriately to the other. Arendt states:

> Forgiving and the relationship it establishes is always an eminently personal (though not necessarily individual or private) affair in which *what* was done is forgiven for the sake of *who* did it. This too, was clearly recognised by Jesus ... and it is the reason for the current conviction that only love has the power to forgive.[13]

Thus forgiveness involves the ability to attend properly to the 'who' of the other and is therefore deeply inter-subjective. Arendt notes that it may not be possible to love everyone but it is possible to *respect* the other and to forgive out of that respect.[14]

Within mothering it is necessary for a mother to acknowledge to her child when she gets things wrong, just as she seeks to teach her child how to admit his failings and take responsibility for his wrongdoings. Mothers can only be 'good enough'. Ruddick suggests that as mothers and children make mistakes, forgive each other and start again, so children develop a moral capacity which enables them to relate well to themselves and others. For clergy the ability to forgive and to be forgiven within the human relationships of the parish is vital for growth, development and maturity. This means developing the humility to admit both genuine failings but also to accept and acknowledge the mistakes in relating made through ignorance or the failure to attend; the ways in which they have trespassed. Too often admitting mistakes or accepting responsibility for things that have generally misfired can be perceived as weakness. Yet, it is through accepting such responsibility that people and situations are freed into new life. At times this means being generous in seeking forgiveness in situations where others may well have

---

[12]   Ibid., p. 240.
[13]   Ibid., p. 241.
[14]   Ibid., p. 243.

overreacted or misunderstood. For a parish priest, in ministering to a large number of very different people, it is almost inevitable that sometimes individuals will be intentionally or unintentionally overlooked, misunderstood or marginalised, and it is important to be able to genuinely recognise their feelings and acknowledge any hurt. To forgive and be forgiven is a *discipline* and it is shaped by the virtues of humility and hopefulness.

Collaborative patterns of ministry that promote mature congregations and communities require the practice of forgiveness; a readiness to admit mistakes and to be hopeful about new beginnings. In mothering we see that apparent failures can be shared as wisdom. They are an aspect of trial-and-error ways of learning. This is not a lesser way of learning; in fact, sometimes it is the only way practice and wisdom can be developed due to the contingency and particularity of human relationships. In parish ministry, mistakes, failures, projects that did not quite work can be regarded as tools for learning and developing wisdom, meaning communities can be kind to each other as they look realistically at why certain things did not work, compassionately naming errors, forgiving mistakes and starting again. This means having the humility to accept our limitations and fallibilities and to continue to respect others despite their fallibility. It also means valuing this way of learning, understanding that learning wisdom through practice is very different from following a set of rules or proscribed behaviours. To accept this means eschewing fantasies of perfection while not letting go of the vision and hope that things can be better and people can flourish.

For Christians the virtue of hope is grounded in the promises of God. It is in hope that we forgive and are forgiven, trusting in the possibilities of redemption and new life both within our earthly relationships and in the eternal realities of God's kingdom. In experiencing God's constant forgiveness and trust in us we find the capacity to continue to forgive and trust others. Hope is intricately linked to the ability to trust in the promises of God and it involves us in learning to trust others and be trustworthy ourselves. Just as we found forgiveness in the philosophies of both Arendt and Ruddick, we find the importance of trust. Arendt sees trust as the faculty to make and keep promises. This, she concludes, requires the virtues of faith and hope.[15] Ruddick identifies the maternal virtues of 'proper trust' and conscientiousness.

In looking at Ruddick's understanding of the virtues of trust and conscientiousness we can find helpful insights for how naming these virtues can help good ministerial practice. She argues that mothers need to both be trustworthy and to trust their emergent child; to be conscientious in helping a child to develop their own conscientiousness. The temptation to a degenerate form of these virtues can lead to giving up on trust and seeking instead blind obedience from their children. Discussions of obedience and conscientiousness inevitably raise issues about how moral values are instilled in children. There are clearly schools of parenting that maintain that strict obedience is the most effective way of instilling appropriate

---

[15]   Arendt, *The Human Condition*, p. 247.

values and shaping a child's life. It is also true that there are theological traditions that would see similar training in obedience as a good model for making disciples. Yet, there is a danger that while these models may help people act appropriately in recognisable circumstances, they may not develop their capacity to deal with new and ambiguous situations where learned rules cannot be easily applied. Blind obedience is not an effective way to develop a child's own conscientiousness. It may not provide him with the capacity to act well in situations that do not fit neatly into the parameters of his upbringing. In terms of discipleship, such models may leave individuals struggling with circumstances that conflict with rigid understandings of right belief. Maturity involves developing the capacity to make good choices in contingent situations, what MacIntyre calls becoming an independent practical reasoner. It links to the Aristotelian virtue of *phronesis*, the intellectual capacity to act virtuously in contingent concrete situations. For people to develop such a capacity, they need to be trusted and helped by those they find trustworthy.

If blind obedience is a degenerate form of proper trust, then it is also important to name the temptation in the other direction. A failure to model values and to challenge behaviour would arise from a lack of conscientiousness on the part of the mother and an abnegation of her responsibility. There are boundaries that need delineating for both safety and acceptability. Failure to take this responsibility, Ruddick suggests, arises out of a lack of confidence in a mother's own sense of values and, therefore, an inability to provide a consistent or robust role model. She becomes inauthentic and does not help her child develop the capacity to discern moral values and make good judgements. Clergy, too, may be tempted to neglect their calling to teach that faith has boundaries – albeit boundaries that can be discussed and explored. The Christian faith involves espousing Christian values and these must be modelled and taught. At their best mothers try to model an authentic and trustworthy way of behaving in the home and the wider world while allowing the kinds of challenging conversations that can enable a child to develop his own sense of authentic behaviour and morality. This authenticity and willingness to allow challenging conversations should be part of good clergy practice.

To be trustworthy and authentic does not rule out conflict. Blind obedience sees conflict as a form of disobedience, challenging the received wisdom, whereas a descent into inauthenticity means that there is no confident place from which to manage conflict and to provide appropriate values with which to judge action. A proper acceptance of the subjectivity of others means that questions and challenges are necessary aspects of developing authenticity and conscientiousness. They are part of the reality of human interaction and the realm of speech that Arendt sees as essential to building up communities. Ruddick writes:

> Her children's differences require the most demanding of a mother's many balancing acts: alongside her own strong convictions of virtues and excellences she is to place her children's human need to ask and answer for themselves

> questions central to moral life ... To judge tenderly yet with confidence is, from
> the earliest years a primary maternal task.[16]

She also notes that this process of learning will inevitably involve feelings of guilt
and shame, which will need forgiveness and hope. It may also involve mothers
having to rethink their own values and admit their own prejudices.

Clearly the maternal task is different from that of ministry, but there are
similarities. Priests need to understand how to foster individual and community
capacities to become mature and this involves both trusting and being trustworthy.
A priest is called to live the Christian life authentically, and has a responsibility to
teach others how to live such a life for themselves. At her ordination she responds
to the question, 'Will you endeavour to fashion your own life and that of your
household according to the way of Christ, that you may be a pattern and example
to Christ's people?' with the words, 'By the help of God, I will.' This is one of
the many promises made that a priest endeavours to keep; the ongoing attempt to
live an authentically Christian life amidst those she cares for. In doing so she is
attempting to be trustworthy.[17] She needs to be open to the challenges and questions
of others, able to reflect on and defend the values by which she lives, and in doing
so help those she cares for develop their Christian conscience and practice.

The calling to lead an authentically Christian life is no different for the priest
than for any Christian, but what is different is the sacramental nature of the priest's
role, which makes her a public sign. Through ordination a priest commits herself
to being a public witness of trustworthiness and faithfulness. Many clergy wear
the clerical collar as a recognition of this sign, an acceptance that they are to be
visible as a Christian presence. Her life is meant to signify the reality of God's
grace and the possibility of living an authentic Christian life. As with mothers, this
is not simply a job or time-limited role. It is a way of being that is consequential
to ordination. There is a level of scrutiny about the lifestyle, and family that would
not be relevant to most other caring professions. There is scrutiny about how a
priest spends her time and her money. As we noted earlier, pastoral encounters are
not all planned. Clergy may be stopped in the supermarket, while walking the dog
or standing at the school gates. In fact, such encounters can often be places of rich
ministry. This means that living authentically has a particularly public element
for parish clergy. Their trustworthiness needs to be manifested by people's ability
to recognise that what they teach is being practised in their own lives. The priest
needs to develop a priestly character, with virtuous habits that mean she is able to
act well contingently. The public scrutiny of a priest's authenticity, like children's
scrutiny of their mothers, means that a priest has to behave in a virtuously Christian
way often enough for people to both trust her judgements and believe that they, too,

---

[16]   Ibid., p. 108.

[17]   Pickard (*Theological Foundations for Collaborative Ministry*, pp. 217–8) connects
ordination to promise-making, drawing on the work of Arendt and Paul Ricouer, *Oneself as
Another*, Chicago and London: University of Chicago Press, 1992.

can live such a virtuous Christian life. They need to be counted on and accountable to the communities they serve, the denominations that have authorised them and, above all, to God, who has called and trusted them to serve faithfully.

Within a given church community others will be sharing in the process of 'growing up into the fullness of Christ' and trying to develop their own authenticity. To facilitate this a priest needs to be a trustworthy listener and also respect the differences of other personalities and experiences. Character is not the same as conformity, and the attempts of others to live virtuous lives may challenge assumptions and open new possibilities for the priest. Yet the priest also has a role in naming what is not good. The description of a priest in the ordinal includes a requirement that they are to admonish. Within her ever-deepening understanding of the Christian faith and her care for people a priest, at times, has to name what is wrong in others; behaviour that is hurtful or unjust. At the same time she has to engage in honest self-reflection. In the demand of 'acceptability' there needs to be a realistic setting of boundaries and a willingness at times to speak out where unacceptable behaviour is manifested. The temptation to be over-critical of others needs to be guarded against, as does the fear of speaking out, which so often leads to a collusion with damaging ways of behaving or a failure to offer guidance to those who are lost. Through growing in virtue a priest learns to speak out of a realistic humility that respects the individuals or communities being spoken to, to judge compassionately and to speak authentically, always being prepared to listen and learn. She also needs to remember that these people entrusted to her care are to be acceptable to God, as she herself needs to be, and that their lives are a witness and sign to others of the way God's grace works in the world. Too often a failure to name and challenge damaging behaviour in church communities at local and wider levels diminishes the witness to the reconciling love of God and the values of the kingdom.

Delighting in the Achievement of Others

The New Testament constantly refers to joy as one of the characteristics of the Christian community. Arendt suggests that joy arises out of relationships of mutual interdependence but Ruddick reminds us that although such joy or as she terms it delight is often spontaneous at other times it needs to be a disciplined response. Therefore she characterises delight as a discipline and virtue. Rejoicing in the successes of one's child is one of the rewarding areas of maternal practice. Some successes are a direct result of gifts that have been deliberately nurtured, but other delights are surprising and personal to that child as they grow into particular skills and abilities that they themselves have developed which may be very different from their parents' experience. However, sometimes it is necessary to delight in the child's successes and pleasures that fall outside one's own particular interests or understanding. Finding ways to acknowledge and delight in the other are essential for the development of the relationship and the love that sustains it. The temptations of perfectionism and competitiveness can make delight difficult. They can lead to over-critical attitudes or an inability to acknowledge the child's own achievements.

The virtue and discipline of delighting in the achievements and development of others should also be a rewarding aspect of parish ministry. Some of this will be easy, especially where people's growth and accomplishments chime with the interests and tastes of the priest, but sometimes it will require discipline to delight in the genuine growth of others and the areas that they excel in. Such delight may mean accommodating practices that would not initially occur to the priest, into the life of the parish. It may divert attention from the priest's own pet projects onto areas that others are taking the initiative in and gaining the glory for. It may also mean allowing people to do things themselves that the priest knows she could do better or quicker.

In practising delight clergy need, like mothers, to resist the temptation to become competitive with their congregation and colleagues. Arrogance that assumes they are the expert or insecurity that finds it difficult to allow others to excel both make it hard for clergy to let people take the initiative or share the strain. Many clergy end up overworking because they find it difficult to let others help or take responsibility for aspects of the work. They can also find it difficult to let others care for them. Perfectionism can also undermine the offerings of others. It is important for clergy to ensure that things are done properly and well, but when perfectionism leads to an over-readiness to criticise and a pickiness with the offerings of others, it limits growth and works against mutuality. Clergy are meant to facilitate and free the gifts of other people in the service of the Church and the kingdom. To do so they need to delight in their achievements, to acknowledge their successes and to sympathise with their failures in ways that encourage new attempts and new directions. Action is creative.

The virtue of delight in Ruddick connects to maternal storytelling, the ways in which mothers help the child to articulate his own story and the ways in which they make sense of their practice through storytelling to others. This relates to Arendt's understanding that action is closely connected to speech. She notes that the realm of work values products and can therefore often dismiss the importance of human speech and storytelling. She comments that they 'will incline to denounce action and speech as idleness, idle busybodyness and idle talk'. Yet it is through the narrating of the ongoing life of the parish that people learn to reflect on what it means to be part of this community. A community with a history and a future shaped by the plurality of people involved. Such stories can find joy in that plurality, celebrating successes and also modelling forgiveness by reflecting on mistakes and failures. Within the Church the ongoing interaction between current narratives of life, community, Biblical stories and Church traditions enables authentically Christian life to be affirmed and judged. Both the formal and informal ways in which stories are told in parishes is vitally important. The latter may at times feel like idle chatter, gossiping and time spent 'unproductively', but it is essential for building up the life of the church, sustaining relationships, promoting reflective ways of learning, affirming achievements and holding out new possibilities.

At one level, all that has been said in this chapter can be seen as obvious. Of course priests need to be attentive, forgiving, caring and compassionate. However, too often these characteristics have been assumed to come automatically through the grace of ordination or simply be part of an individual's personality. What I am stressing is that character is learned through practice. And the desirable characteristics of a parish priest need to be better articulated so that reflection can lead to good practice and to a sharing of good practice. Where the language to value good practice is not easily available much of what matters can be dismissed as 'doing nothing'.

Good practice is learned in relationship. It is in and through the relationships of priest to people and communities that the character of that priest is shaped and honed, just as the community's character is shaped by the myriad of different individuals who play their part, including the priest. This development of character does not negate the grace of God working in a priest's life; it is about learning to recognise that grace and to enhance the opportunities for its outworking in the community served. Grace is necessary for priests, as for all Christians, to help in resisting temptations, developing virtues, enabling forgiveness for failings and providing the hope necessary to continue. Yet grace does not preclude the hard work of learning and developing the ways of thinking and feeling that enable clergy to respond well to the contingent circumstances and real people entrusted to their care. Collaborative relationships do not just happen and we need to be careful that initiatives that are intended to help clergy in their ministry do not unintentionally damage generative creative power-sharing. Building up community, helping individuals and congregations to mature, caring for those in distress and delighting in the achievements of others does not lend itself to easily measurable targets. Yet, as in maternal care, the signs of good practice can be seen in the flourishing of those cared for, in their increasing ability to grow up into themselves, and as Christians into the fullness of Christ.

Chapter 9
Using Maternal Language to Articulate Aspects of Parish Ministry: Some Examples

In previous chapters I have said that it is not helpful to reduce mothering or ministry to a list of tasks. Instead the skills developed are as much about attitudes and ways of being as they are about what is done. However, I have also suggested that there are skills that clergy develop which often go unrecognised, unarticulated and thus unvalued. Drawing on the experience and language of mothering, I will suggest a number of different terms that can articulate some of these skills. This is not meant to be a full account of ministerial skills, just hopefully a pointer to ways of naming aspects of ministry that may help priests find ways themselves of naming what they do. Stadlen maintains that if mothers do not have a language to describe meaningfully the activity that takes up their time and energy, they dismiss it as *nothing*.[1] There is a danger that clergy do the same. So in this chapter I will look at some aspects of ministry that are assumed to be instinctual, incidental or 'nothing much'. In naming and affirming such activity I maintain that such good practice can be learned and improved.

The Art of Cherishing

One of the assumptions made about mothering is that mothers cherish their children out of a profound almost mystical mother-love. In looking at mothering, I noted that this love is not automatic. There will, for most mothers, be many times when it is easy and rewarding to cherish her child but also times when it is difficult; where the response can feel more dutiful than joyful. To cherish means to hold something as precious and sometimes that involves looking beyond the immediate moment, drawing on the long-term relationship in expectation of its ongoing rewards. It also means recognising that the child is at some level a gift as well as a responsibility.[2] Cherishing involves both an attitude and practical expressions of that attitude. To be cherished is to feel cared for and valued. It is also to *be* cared for.

---

[1]   Stadlen, *What Mothers Do*, see especially pp. 19–26.

[2]   Bonnie Miller-McLemore reflects on the Christian understanding of children as gifts in *Let the Children Come* (San Francisco 2003). She maintains that it is because children are gifts that there is an ongoing responsibility to them, they require 'unearned gifting', p. 102. She writes, 'In other words, the gift of children involves paradoxically a corresponding and sometimes costly duty,' p. 104.

Parish ministry is about cherishing the people God has given and, through doing so, helping them to know that they are precious. Cherishing requires attentiveness and it requires the ability to recognise that though we might not find it easy to love everyone in our care, they are all at some level a gift from God. So, parish priests need to practise an attitude of valuing people as God's gift to this place and this church. Some are easy to cherish because knowing and loving them is rewarding, and their help and support are clear gifts which are easy to thank God for. But it is also important to learn to cherish the difficult people, the marginalised and the ones who, for whatever reason, are annoying. This is not to deny the reality of one's feelings or to fail to acknowledge that some people are actually difficult and some unlovely. It is to take seriously the Church as the Body of Christ in which all members matter and to take the responsibility for the cure of souls, which is not limited to the easy ones. In my experience, learning to find ways in which the people I found difficult enhanced the ministry of the parish was an important practice and one that I could consciously improve. By recognising individuals as a gift to the particular parish and ministry, I learned to acknowledge that some challenged me to concern myself with issues or areas I would otherwise neglect. Some taught me to find new ways of seeing people and new ways of valuing people, challenging my own and others' prejudices. Others simply encouraged me to pray and to trust God.

In any church community there will be some people who do not feel cherished beyond the church. These may include people who are lonely and unloved, who have lost loved ones or who have found life disappointing. One of the responsibilities of the parish priest is to find ways to particularly cherish these people. Fears about the decline of church attendance amongst younger generations can sometimes imply that the elderly who come to church are not that important. Yet they are gifts of God, often rich in prayer and wisdom, kindness and faithfulness. Priests often find that these are the people who care for her and sustain her in prayer. Simple things like calling people by name, remembering previous conversations and particular interests can matter immensely. It is a discipline and a skill to learn to remember such details. Like all skills, some will find it easier to master than others. Developing techniques that aid memory, writing notes, using trusted people to fill in forgotten details can all help in the process of making people feel cherished.

As a curate our training incumbent expected us, by the end of our first year, to be able to name each person as we gave them Communion. There were usually about 150–200 communicants on a Sunday. He did not ask if we were good at learning names, he simply assumed that we would find a way to learn. His reason was that there was not always time to speak to everyone after the service, but through this naming at the Communion rail, each one had been recognised and, at a simple level, cherished. It also meant we concentrated on who was there, noted newcomers and visitors and found opportunities to talk to them. Another example reminds us that clergy can find ways of sharing the cherishing of people through developing good systems of cherishing. Again during my time as a curate, the Bishop of St Albans used to write to every member of the clergy the week before their parish came up in the prayer diary, asking if they had any specific requests for prayer. I assume he had a good secretary who kept the diary, produced the letters and collated the responses, but that did not detract from my sense of being cherished and personally prayed for.

The importance of cherishing is a corrective to ideas that detachment is a necessary attitude to parishioners. There is within the Christian tradition an understanding of *agape* as selfless love, and this has sometimes led to a privileging of detachment. Yet, as we have already noted, there is a difference between a care that temporarily focuses away from oneself onto the other, and detachment. Love and care is always hoping for a response, for reciprocity and a desire to deepen the relationship; it is not detached.[3] The way of Christ involves self-giving and suffering but these are not ends in themselves. They are expressions of a love that desires relationship, which longs to draw people deeper into knowledge and life with Him. Detachment from people is therefore not a good discipline for a ministry that needs to maintain multiple ways of strengthening and sustaining human relationships. There is, however, a discipline involved in ensuring that, as far as it is possible, *all* feel cherished. Therefore the easy relationships must not be allowed to degenerate into cliques and inner circles that exclude others.

The Art of Comforting

One of the ways that mothers cherish their children is through comforting them. The ability to comfort a baby is one of the earliest skills that a mother has to learn. It involves generic ways of being and behaving, but is always focused on the concrete reality of the person and the situation. It is learned through practice. Comforting involves the art of assuring another that, despite the sense of distress they feel, they will not be overcome. It involves the ability to be compassionate, to feel with the one who is distressed and through touch, speech and visual signals to model a calmness that doesn't invalidate the distress but affirms the ability to carry on living through it. It is the process by which we help another to rediscover their equilibrium, restoring them to a place where they can manage themselves.

If we look at an example from mothering, we see the kinds of thought and action involved in comforting. When a child falls and grazes his knee, he wants comforting. His mother will probably comfort physically, holding the child; she will also speak to the child, acknowledging that grazed knees hurt, that when you hurt you often cry, that bleeding is frightening and that the garden path suddenly seems a more threatening place. She will also reassure him that the bleeding

---

[3]   See Christine Gudorf, 'Parenting Mutual Love and Sacrifice', in B.H. Andolsen et al. (eds), *Women's Consciousness, Women's Conscience* (Minneapolis 1985), pp. 175–91. In this article she reflects on her parenting of her severely disabled children. She writes, 'Christian love should not be constructed as disinterested or set apart from other love as essentially self-sacrificing. All love both involves sacrifice and aims at mutuality,' p. 185.

will stop, that he will soon recover and that he will run and fall and run again. She will probably do this alongside practical thought and action, cleaning the wound, assessing whether it needs further attention or just a snazzy plaster. If his injury is far worse and she is uncertain of the future, she will continue to comfort him as she does all that is practical to protect him. The child is helped to cope with the immediate overwhelming emotions. He may recover very quickly and run off to play some more or he may need ongoing attention and affirmation. Through comforting, his mother has helped him to cope with what was, at the time, frightening and distressing. Comforting involves physical body language, a particular tone of voice that soothes and reassures and an ability on the mother's part to control her own fear and feelings so that she can *de-stress* the child.

Comforting is different from counselling. It is about dealing with the immediacy of feelings rather than trying to help someone reflect on and unpick such feelings. The primary human need in the face of events that cause distress is for comforting; counselling is a later possibility when the initial trauma has passed and individuals may need help in making sense of what they have been through. Comforting involves assuring the person that what they are experiencing, though it feels overwhelming, is within the normal spectrum of reactions to the circumstances they face. The etymological root of the word comforting is 'to give strength', and Stadlen writes:

> Human comfort is one of the finest strengths that we offer each other. It can be casually given, by a touch, a smile, a few words or even by silence. Yet it's very effective. It doesn't usually alter the source of our troubles, but it strengthens us so we feel better able to confront them.[4]

Comforting, she states is 'very effective'.

This needs to be owned and affirmed by clergy because, in the myriad of pastoral encounters that make up parish ministry, they are constantly called upon to comfort people. In maternal comforting mothers attend over time to the particularities of their child and learn ways of comforting that are appropriate to him. Clergy, in many encounters, do not have the luxury of an ongoing relationship. This means they need to develop a very keen ability to 'read' people and comfort appropriately. This is a skill and a discipline which, again, will come easier to some than others and will feel more 'natural' in some circumstances than others. It requires the ability to use feelings to both assess appropriate action and evaluate it. Experience of the practice builds wisdom and can begin to make this reading and assessing almost second nature. It requires the kind of thinking that Ruddick attributes to mothers, where 'feeling, thinking and action are conceptually linked'.[5]

Comforting is an embodied skill that often involves touch. For mothers it frequently means physical holding. Clearly this is inappropriate where there is not

---

[4]   Stadlen, *What Mothers Do*, p. 60.
[5]   Ruddick, *Maternal Thinking*, p. 70.

already a close relationship, but comforting still needs to be embodied, even if that is a simple touch or sitting or standing in a way that inclines towards the one in need. The art of comforting involves drawing on one's own experiences of feeling in need of comfort and of being comforted. Aspects of this require empathy – that is, to relate from one's own experiences to the emotional state of another.[6] Yet it often requires more than empathy, as a priest has to deal with emotions and feelings that she has not had herself. It also requires perspective. De Marneffe writes:

> A mother's responsiveness combines both her willingness to enter into emotional states with her child – what we commonly call empathy – and her ability to reflect and offer a different perspective ... Thus, in the everyday act of comforting her child, a mother's very ability to help her child depends, fundamentally, on her having her own different perspective.[7]

It is this combination of being able to recognise and validate another's feelings while also being able to offer perspective that makes comforting effective. In good practice, clergy will be able to make people feel comfortable and to offer comfort. In all situations of need they will listen and attend in order to acknowledge feelings, but they will not themselves be overwhelmed by the feelings. They will be reflecting on any practical ways forward and holding onto their own sense of hope for these people and this situation. An aspect of that hope is the reality of God, so they also hold such people before God in prayer.

An example where comforting is the principal skill that clergy need to use is in the common pastoral encounter of bereavement. When people are bereaved they need to have the pain acknowledged, to have their feelings of loss and sorrow recognised and validated. They need to know that grief hurts, it is all right to cry, it will be physically tiring and it is confusing. They need someone who is calm to speak to them about the landscape of grief, the ways in which you forget for a moment and then are brought up short with the memory of loss, and how the world can suddenly seem a more frightening place because doctors do not know how to make everyone better and God did not answer your prayers. At this point they need comforting, not counselling. They need the practical arrangements to be intermingled with the soothing reassurance that this can be endured, however impossible it feels.

The comfort that clergy are offering is both a human concern for people in distress but it is also a compassionate witness to the love of God. Clergy are able, in themselves, to trust that although they may not know the individuals, God does.

---

6   Noddings, Ruddick and Miller-McLemore all discuss the use of the word empathy for this feeling with others and suggest that what is required is more than empathy. All suggest that empathy implies understanding another's feelings by identifying them as like one's own. See Noddings, *Caring*, pp. 30–31; Ruddick, *Maternal Thinking*, p. 121; Bonnie Miller-McLemore, *In the Midst of Chaos* (San Francisco 2007), p. 52.

7   de Marneffe, *Maternal Desire*, p. 79.

Thus in attending to the people, a priest is also attending to God, praying that in them and through them God's grace may flow. Because they are comforting as a priest and are recognised as a representative of the Church, their words, actions and presence bear witness to Christ. Therefore, their comforting is also prophetic; it speaks of the values of the kingdom and proclaims the love of God for these particular human beings. The concrete situation and the particular people will dictate how the priest articulates this prophetic dimension, but even where words are few, the act of being there and offering comfort as a witness of the Church speaks of God's love. Compassion and attentive love are virtues necessary for comforting and so is the virtue of hope. To comfort others is always to hold before them the hope of new beginnings and new possibilities.

Like many clergy, I learned the art of comforting through watching the way an experienced priest comforted and cared. I learned from his ability to articulate and reflect on what he was doing and why. And alongside this I drew on my own experiences of being comforted and not being comforted, utilising feelings as a way of judging action. I also drew on my sense of God as comforter through both personal experiences and the teachings of Christian faith. Reflection and practice can, in time, lead to a seemingly natural ability to read people and respond appropriately, but there is a danger that if the practice is not named then it is not valued. Good comforting, like good caring, is confirmed in the reception of those receiving it. Many individuals recognise the generosity of such comforting and are grateful to be skilfully cared for. Like mothers, priests are expected to be good at it, so a failure to learn and an inability to read people and comfort them appropriately when they turn to the Church for help can damage people's trust in the Church and even distort their understanding of God.

Yet, because 'comfortable' and 'comforting' are words that connect to cosiness and sentimentality, there is ambivalence in owning comforting as a primary ministerial practice. Sentimentality, though, is not comforting; it is a form of 'cheery denial', which Ruddick identifies as a degenerate form of the virtue of cheerfulness or hope. Comforting is not sentimental; it acknowledges the reality of pain and fear.[8] The association of comforting with the maternal, and thus with dependency and vulnerability, has meant that it is undervalued and not recognised as a skill. The increasing professionalism of counselling has added to the undervaluing of the very different, non-professional skill of comforting. Counselling is a particular and valuable practice, but clergy need to acknowledge confidently that in parish ministry they fulfil a very different role from counsellors. Articulating the particular skills involved in comforting, in meeting the distressed in the midst of distress and helping them practically, emotionally and spiritually to move through it, is important if clergy are to value their own abilities and feel that others recognise comforting as an art and skill. In speaking about pastoral ministry there needs to be resistance to eliding comforting and counselling or of privileging the latter over the former.

---

[8] de Marneffe, *Maternal Desire*, discusses the sentimentalised view of mothering, pp. 144–5.

Embodied Ways of Knowing and Communicating

I noted above that comforting was an embodied practice and many aspects of cherishing are as well. They involve both the use of body language and the ability to read it in others. This kind of communicating is essential in maternal practice because the early stages of the relationship are developed before the child can speak, but they continue to be central to the ongoing relationship of mother and child. And because this is how we learn to relate, they continue to matter in adult relationships. The tone of voice used to reassure, soothe or welcome can be as important as any words spoken. As can the tone of disapproval and the admonitory look. Appropriate levels of touching, a hand on the arm or, if the relationship is right, a hug can convey real sympathy or warmth. Eye contact and bodily attention all speak to people at a deep level.

In mothering a young baby this non-verbal, embodied communication is highlighted because there is, as yet, no speech. Yet as children develop speech, the non-verbal ways of communicating do not cease. Over time, ways of bodily communicating develop in a good relationship and children of varying ages may look for the reassuring nod or the affirming touch. Body language is important and different cultures can have very different attitudes to eye contact, touch and voice tone. This is why understanding the context of ministry is so important. Clergy need to be self-reflective about the messages they convey through non-verbal signals, just as they need to become practised in reading the body language of others. This is all part of the attention talked about in preceding chapters. In individual encounters compassion, interest, patience and attention are conveyed in embodied ways that often matter far more than the actual words. Yet they need to relate to the words authentically.

Emphasising the non-verbal ways in which humans communicate through body language and symbolic spaces and objects is not intended to detract from the importance of speech. It is through speaking and storytelling that people make meaning of their own lives and the lives of others. Such stories make sense of the symbols and rituals that shape both homes and communities. Even before children learn to talk, mothers – alongside the non-verbal communication – talk to and with their child. It is the proper integration of the verbal and the non-verbal that enables children to learn their 'mother' tongue.

For those coming new to Christianity and the worshipping life of the Church, the priest is often the one who shapes 'the mother tongue': how they speak of and practise the faith. Whatever the particular tradition of a church, the worshipping experience will involve not just the spoken words, but the unspoken language of voice tone and posture alongside deliberate embodied practices. These will be shaped by theological and doctrinal beliefs as well as matters of style, taste and habit. People will stand at some points, sit or kneel at others. They may cross themselves or raise their arms in the air. In doing so they are adopting postures and movements that have become part of their worship. For newcomers and outsiders such movements may seem strange, but for the regular worshippers they are habitual and almost unthinking. They have been learned; deliberately taught or simply copied. They become the habitus of that community,[9] the mother tongue of faith. They have parallels with the manners learned at home: how to eat at table, handle the cutlery, greet visitors and behave in public. Mothers help to create the habitus of a home, teaching such embodied ways of being through deliberate repetition and correction as well as through modelling behaviour. Thus my own children stand up to greet a visitor who comes into the room and move to shake hands, offer accepted words of greeting. These learned bodily movements happen on most occasions without a deliberate thought because they have become habitual. They have watched over the years how adults behave, they have been formally told what to do, but now the movements are a 'natural' response to the presence of a visitor.

At home and in church such embodied practices will be shaped by cultural understandings of normal behaviour and particular preferences of this place and these people. While mothers shape children from their earliest years, clergy move in to existing congregations and may find some of the postures and movements do not correspond to their own habitual practice. Understanding how deeply embodied ways of doing things affect people is important in understanding when and how changes can be made. It is also important in the clergy role of both deliberately teaching postures and movements and modelling them when presiding at services. In both a home and a church there will be an accepted way of doing things that simply seems to be normal to those who belong. In the home, mothers have a pivotal role in creating this habitus and in a particular church the incumbent is similarly pivotal.[10]

It therefore matters how the priest inhabits her role. The tone of voice, the eye contact, the level of attention and presence will all speak to those participating as loudly as the actual words. The conviction that can be read in the non-verbal language of a priest will make a difference to how trustworthy and believable the words being proclaimed are. This can be particularly important for newcomers and visitors, who take their cues from the priest. The physical actions of those leading the service should provide clues to the newcomer but not distract from the flow. The priest needs to be able to explain why certain movements and actions happen when they do. Thus they need to be able to reflect on their own as well as their

---

[9]   The concept of *habitus* comes from Mauss, *The Notion of Body Techniques in Sociology and Psychology*. Davison and Milbank, *For the Parish*, define it as 'the embodied daily performance of beliefs and traditions that are acted rather than conceptualised' and they link this to the ongoing work of the Holy Spirit in a church community, pp. 141–2.

[10]   Martin Stringer, *On the Perception of Worship: The Ethnography of Worship in Four Christian Congregations in Manchester* (Birmingham: 1999), provides a fascinating study of the language and practice of four different congregations. It highlights how bodily practices as well as phraseology become almost unthinking to the regular members as they express their faith through the embodied and linguistic practices that are habitual to the congregation.

congregation's style. The importance of the non-verbal and its integration with the verbal may seem a very obvious aspect of ministry. However, if it is not named and explored it can be dismissed as unimportant. In naming this integration as a skill I am also pointing out that it can be developed and improved, which means that clergy need others who can sensibly comment on how they appear *bodily* when conducting worship and pastoral encounters.

Multitasking and Multi-Attending

The examples above have stressed the importance of clergy being able to attend properly to the particularity of the other. In fact, clergy need to develop the capacity to be attending to and reading the body language of others while carrying on with other tasks of ministry. It is often acknowledged that one skill-set that mothers develop is the ability to multitask. This is usually understood at two levels. Firstly mothers learn to be able to do more than one thing at a time, for example, they can feed a baby, cook a meal and assist an older child with homework *simultaneously*. The other meaning of multitasking is that they need to be able to turn their hand to lots of different tasks in any given day, switching between different roles from play companion to domestic worker, to skilled negotiator, without even factoring in any work beyond the home. Both aspects of multitasking are, I would suggest, part of the practice of parish ministry. Clergy are less likely to be doing two or three tasks at the same time, but they do, like mothers, learn to be multi-attending. That is, while fully engaged on one task, they may be attending on a number of different levels. A good example of this is when a priest is conducting worship on a Sunday morning.

The primary task on such an occasion for the priest is to conduct the worship well. As we noted above, this involves appropriately performing the rites of the given tradition using words, gestures and movement in such a way that the worshipping experience of all the people is meaningful and the whole is an acceptable offering to God. In thinking about comforting above, I commented that the dual aspect of the one comforting is essential to the process: that is, the ability to feel with the person but not to be so caught up in their feelings that the necessary perspective is lost. There is a similar need for a dual perspective in leading worship. The ability for a priest to be attentively present in any service or ritual is a subtly different experience from an individual themselves getting caught up in the worship. For a priest, however strongly a particular religious ritual touches their own worshipping self, must, if presiding, be consciously attending to the others. She thus learns to balance a genuine worshipping experience with a *responsive* attitude to the congregation and all that is going on.

As she leads the worship she is unobtrusively scanning the congregation to see who is there and how people are. She will make mental notes of certain absences with connected planned actions: to make enquiries, or pay a visit or make a call. She will take note of any newcomers or infrequent visitors and again begin to think of actions. Newcomers may prompt subtle adjustments to the service, a clearer indication of how the service flows or a particular word of welcome. She will notice that the body language of someone suggests that there are issues that need following up and note that the particular readings may be hard for someone else.

She may also be attending to the roles others play in the service. There will be aspects of training that require sensitive feedback. Others need affirmation and thanks for the parts they have played in the worship, whether visible or behind the scenes. She may be assessing for herself how changes in liturgy, choreography or use of space feel and function. She is also offering her own worship, trying to attend to God's message for herself and this community, to discern the way forward and the right priorities. All of this is unobtrusive. It is a form of attending to the concrete reality of this congregation as they are this morning and certainly should not intrude on their worshipping experience. It is a form of attentive love that mentally asks if all is well with these people and how best she and they can, collectively, be the church they are called to be. This attention feeds into the priest's experience of presiding over the worship of the community and into her own prayer that she may be able to minister to them by the grace of God.

Such unobtrusive attention is part of an ongoing habit of parish ministry as the priest chairs meetings, joins in the toddler group and participates in parish events. She scans the people and reads the non-verbal signs. It often goes hand in hand with a form of praying that mentally holds the people encountered and met before God. This kind of prayer is unobtrusive and mostly unarticulated. The attention can allow the priest to recognise and respond to the needs of the other even if, at times, the other does not know how to articulate them or doesn't have the courage to share them. If practised, it results in a sensitivity that can feel changes in conversations, read signs in people's bodies and respond appropriately.

Multitasking and multi-attending in parish ministry involves the ability to move emotionally from very different environments and situations without bringing inappropriate attitudes into each. Martyn Percy refers to this as the 'enormous range of temperatures that a priest experiences and moves through in a given day',[11] moving from rain to sunshine, from formal to relaxed and warm. The patchwork nature of a priest's daily diary means that she can move from comforting a widow straight into singing time with the toddlers. She may then have a few visits, some to people who are a delight, others who are bitter or boring individuals who sap her energy. The day may include meetings both within the church and in organisations in the wider community where she represents the church. At some of these she will need to be assertive in stating a position, at others simply listen and show her face. Meanwhile she is waiting for the phone to ring because a faithful soul is dying and that might mean a reorganisation of the whole diary. It may also mean the loss of someone special to her and the community. In her head are the readings for

---

[11]   In conversation, January 2011, and see M. Percy, *The Ecclesial Canopy: Faith, Hope, Charity* (Farnham 2012).

Sunday's sermon, the plans for a Lent talk, how to respond to the latest diocesan initiative and whether she has time to go to the shops to stock up the fridge.

These encounters need to be contained at some level. In each place she must attend to what is happening. She must listen attentively to the widow and then move on to laugh with the children while picking up on the tentative questions of faith expressed by one of the mums. She must do her best to attend to those she likes and those she finds hard and in the meetings play her part with integrity. It all involves an ability to move from one thing to another in a way that continues to hold all that is important while switching her focus onto the real and concrete. This multi-attending is a skilful practice that good clergy develop so that it seems to come easily but, again, I would suggest that an inability to name it can mean that even those who do it do not recognise and value it.

The patchwork nature of the clergy diary also points to the way that clergy straddle two very different ways of understanding time. Here again I think there are interesting parallels with mothering. A parish priest lives in the real world with its linear patterns of time. She makes appointments and schedules meetings and has an outline of a normal working day. Yet she is also dealing with the unplanned and the unpredictable. People get ill and die unexpectedly, people feel a desire to speak of issues that can lead to explorations of faith at unpredictable moments and none of this takes account of the planned diary. Clergy therefore have to work with both the planned and the unplanned, allowing space for the unexpected and accepting that sometimes everything will come at once and seem utterly overwhelming. Most clergy accept this and are good at managing the overwhelming, but they also need to learn to accept the unplanned periods of quiet and rejoice in them as times to recharge and relax. The linear pattern of time means that we can feel guilty resting or relaxing in what is designated as working hours but if we acknowledge that the 'work' demanded doesn't always conform to these hours then it can perhaps be easier to let go of the guilt in the times when things slacken off for a bit. Mothers of babies and young children can feel the benefits of resting when the baby sleeps, putting their feet up while the toddler is absorbed in a new toy or enjoying a relaxing coffee and chat while her child plays with another's. Clergy need to accept the slack times as gifts to allow for relaxation and refreshment even when they are not days off.

Mothers can also learn to slow down and move sometimes at the child's pace, dawdling along the road studying the plants in the wall or standing watching a digger on the building site. Children can teach her about living in the present moment, enjoying the simplicity of things and the joy of now. Practising this ability not to rush enables clergy to focus on the unexpected encounters, to allow time to look and to listen, to people, to places and, above all, to God. My training incumbent encouraged me to walk as much as possible around the parish, allowing enough time between appointments to stop and chat if necessary, or to walk down a different road and reflect on the people there. For many the sheer size of the parishes in their care makes this impossible, but finding the ways to create a slower pace in the midst of all the busyness of parish life is an important practice for allowing people and God to interrupt the careful planning. Clergy need to find a balance between being seen as approachable, with time to talk, and managing all the many tasks expected of them. Accepting the unpredictable periods of busyness and calm and finding ways to weave them in to the ongoing linear demands of ordinary time is a necessary adaptation to the practice of ministry, which differs in so many ways from the measurable productivity of other patterns of working life.

Homemaking and Housekeeping

At the centre of parish ministry is the local church building. In the last chapter it was noted that maintenance and care of these buildings was a central part of parish ministry. This involved much of the 'labouring' aspects of the role, which can be understood as housekeeping. Buildings need to be regularly cleaned and tidied. They need to be repaired and sometimes reordered. Spaces outside need grass mowing, weeds dug up and litter removed. All of this can and should be undertaken collectively, but it must be done. Ruddick sees a home as central to maternal practice and she links it to the skill of administration.[12] This is a term that is more familiar to clergy than it is to most mothers, but unpacking what it means in maternal practice can provide a more holistic way of viewing it in ministry.

The management of a home requires administrative skills. It requires the planning of meals and other necessary domestic chores. Food must be bought, budgeted for, cooked and served. Different needs of family members must be factored in, allowing for likes and dislikes. Social diaries need to be coordinated, events need to be organised; time for holidays, appointments and general relaxing need to be fitted around different work and school patterns. This is all carried out within a family constantly adapting to change. Children grow and need new clothes, new toys, different space and different activities. Careful thought needs to go into what is retained and what discarded so that the home doesn't become overwhelmed with clutter. As children become more mature, they can participate in the collective chores, but that often means more supervision and constructive feedback. Thus homemaking involves both housekeeping, in the sense of domestic chores, and also managing budgets, administration and overseeing those who help in the domestic tasks. It also involves strategising and planning for all the changes of a growing community.

This has strong parallels with the domestic, administrative and management aspects of parish ministry. The regular 'domestic' tasks of church life can be shared, but must be done, requiring some level of oversight, affirmation and constructive feedback. The administrative and management tasks can and should be carried out collaboratively. Overseeing the collective 'domestic' labour of church life and the administrative aspects involves priests in management. Alongside this

---

[12]   Ruddick, *Maternal Thinking*, p. 87.

management are the strategic aspects of planning for the future and adapting for change, which is a consequence of growing changing people.

In both maternal homemaking and parish management what is essentially important is the motivation for the administrative tasks. These places, the home and the local church, are there to provide real people with the physical, emotional and spiritual space that underpins their growing in faith and flourishing as Christians. These places are shaped by the threefold demands of nurturing towards maturity. They must have a sense of security and familiarity that enables those who belong to feel held and safe. They need to allow for growth and change, so they must have levels of flexibility. They also have to be socially acceptable – which means they must be recognisable for those who come in from outside – while witnessing to the values and beliefs espoused by those who belong.

In a domestic home there needs to be enough that is familiar, making it a comfortable and safe space for its inhabitants. When moving house, there is always a sense of relief when certain key pieces of furniture, pictures and objects are put in place. This new space now feels like our space. The familiar needs to be maintained alongside flexibility and change. Changes will be dictated by the different needs of the growing children; from playrooms, to teenage 'snug' and from endless toys to computers, drum kits and quantities of long-limbed friends. The home must accommodate different people under the same roof and, at best, be a place of hospitality to outsiders. In order to be hospitable there are cultural norms about how space is used and acceptable levels of order and disorder. Clearly, wealth, physical space, size of family and all sorts of cultural assumptions will affect homemaking. Poor housing and lack of money make the task of homemaking particularly difficult. Yet, an over-obsession with fashion or a preciousness about all the contents can make a well-appointed home unwelcoming and unhomely.

Clergy share with others in the care of buildings that are often complex and expensive to manage. Difficult decisions need to be made about how they are to be maintained, heated, cleaned and utilised. They contain many artefacts that resonate with the people who come, and these artefacts make them feel at home, but it is not always the same things that people love and value. Changes in need raise complex questions about reordering the space. People are no longer used to sitting in cold buildings or walking miles to the nearest toilet. Historical significance and community memories play into the way buildings are valued and cared for. There is also the important sense that changes that seem good at the moment may simply lead to problems for the future, when tastes and attitudes will have shifted again in ways we cannot predict.

The ability to manage all of this well is part of the priest's role, but it must be remembered that the role of manager arises out of the responsibility to care for the people and places; it should not be the primary model. It is also clear that it involves the ability to balance the competing 'goods' of the practice and to facilitate change in collaborative and constructive ways. Administration and management are necessary tools for homemaking and housekeeping. They are necessary tools for caring for both a church building and the community for whom that space exists. Poor administration means that people and events can get forgotten. Poor housekeeping means that cluttered and dirty spaces make people feel unwelcome and unvalued. Unkempt spaces speak of neglect and in a church they are dishonouring, not just to the congregation, but also to God. Poor planning means that necessary bills cannot be paid, affecting repair, maintenance and good stewardship of resources. Clergy need, with others, to oversee the care of the spaces entrusted to them. This can often be an onerous aspect of the work, taking up time and energy with little to show for all the hard work. It requires skills that can be developed and practised. At its best it is seamless, happening in ways that do not distract those who come from their primary task of worshipping God.

Weaning and Managing Change

As noted above, housekeeping and homemaking involves the management of change. Like mothers, clergy are engaged in the care of real people so they will consistently need to facilitate change. Some aspects of change are negotiated with ease and it is only when looking back that the extent of adaptation is fully perceived, but some change needs managing. One of the primary changes in a young child's life is moving from milk to solid food, and this process is named weaning.

When a baby or young child is weaned from breast or bottle they not only give up a familiar form of food but also the process of being closely held. If a mother is breastfeeding, the baby has a fair amount of autonomy in how much milk he ingests and the balance between fore and hind milk. He could decide on whether this was a quick feed or a long, slow experience. In moving onto solids he gains many things, including a more varied and satisfying diet, but he loses the holding, the autonomy and the familiar comfort. The mother, too, is involved in both freedoms and losses. In weaning her child she can let others share in the task of feeding; she will be able to leave the baby for longer, perhaps return to work outside the home. Yet she is giving up the easy, free and portable source of food for a process of cooking, processing or buying suitable baby food. Mealtimes are no longer a quiet time of holding, but are now messy and sometimes fraught.

The wisdom of maternal practice has taught mothers that the process of weaning needs to be planned and managed. It has to acknowledge both the excitement of the new and the fears and challenges of letting go of old ways of doing things. Weaning involves gradually introducing new tastes without immediately withdrawing the milk. It requires a deliberate attempt to be relaxed on the mother's part, especially when lovingly prepared food is rejected. It requires creativity and perseverance. A mother must try and see the change from the child's perspective, to recognise the reality of their fears and to address them as best they can. These fears may seem bizarre and illogical to an outsider, but are connected to the meanings the child has created around his world. A mother also needs to be honest about her own feelings and reasons for choosing how and when to introduce change.

Mothers learn that the process of weaning a child from milk to solids is replicated in so many other areas of the child's life. A child is weaned from a cot to a bed, from favourite toys to new ones, from the safety of nursery to the infant school, and so it proceeds. If a child has had change managed well in the early years he should, hopefully, find it easier to embrace and manage changes himself. The process of weaning in all its forms involves trial and error and learning from the successes and failures of other practitioners. It involves focusing on the particular child with his individual likes and fears. In some cases reaction to a suggested change may result in a rethink about whether that particular change needs to happen at this time and at this pace: could it be re-imagined? Creative ways of retaining aspects of the past can be incorporated in to the new, for example by periods of quiet physical holding being included in the rituals of the day when the actual physical process of breastfeeding is stopped.[13] Again, assessing feelings and recognising the reality of the other can reduce conflict and encourage a shared ownership of changes. Inherent in the process of weaning is an understanding that change involves letting go of valued things which may carry resonances beyond their obvious utility.

Managing change in parish life is often complex and contested. Thus reflecting on weaning can offer insights. Clergy need to appreciate that people's attachment to certain objects or ways of doing things may be for many different reasons, thus the fears of change work at levels that are not immediately obvious. Altering the familiar words of a service can cause upset not because of changed meaning but due to a change of rhythm or the loss of certain phrases that reassure and console. Objects in the church that seem of little use can hold particular memories for some that connect them to people or events in the past. Changing the familiar things may connect to fears about ageing, lack of worth, loneliness and even issues about death. Things may well look very different from the pews than from the pulpit

This means that when things are changed, even when the reasons for change seem straightforward and good, some people may find letting go difficult because of the particular way they resonate with an object or practice. Because many of the attachments people have to objects, the use of space and ways of worshipping function at a semiotic level, they are not easy to articulate. This means that people may react in ways that seem illogical to others, including the vicar. Contested power and the possibility of conflict will be an inevitable aspect of any community. What is important is to ensure that they do not become destructive. For a community to continue to flourish and grow, changes will inevitably need to happen. Decisions have to be negotiated that lead to appropriate action or inaction and choices between priorities must be made. Trying to understand things from different perspectives can allow the priest to recognise the deeply held concerns of the other, even if these are quite alien to her. It can also allow for others to delight

---

[13] Psalm 131 offers the image of 'a weaned child on its mother's breast' as a picture of the soul resting on God. The image suggests how the holding is maintained as a restful, secure place even when the child has moved beyond the physical necessity of breastfeeding.

in things the priest finds kitsch or unattractive. Finding ways to address the real fears behind change, to present new things creatively and to negotiate a process can reduce conflict.

Clergy, like mothers, also have to look honestly at their reasons for changing things or resisting change. Is this about making her own life easier, a matter of her personal taste or the assumption that experts, offering generic patterns and timetables for change, know what is best? Unlike mothers, clergy also have to acknowledge that they are passing through; they will in due course leave whilst many of the congregation stay. Thus they have a special obligation not to impose their own particular likes and dislikes. They also have a responsibility for the whole community and therefore must try and see things from a number of different angles. At times this means a priest letting go of her own pet projects and ideas. Success is not about getting her own way, but about helping the community to grow up in ways that continue to preserve people's faith and that are acceptable to the wider Church and, above all, to God. To let go of an issue gracefully may enable growth in others of a far richer quality than anything she might have planned; it requires the virtue of humility.

Negotiating change in a community inevitably means that some will at times feel hurt, misunderstood and overlooked and such people need continuing compassion and care. Centrally important is the realisation that the process matters. In managing change in communities the ends never justify the means. The process may not necessarily arrive at the ends in the way expected, but if there is integrity in the process, the end will be one that many can own. It may even be, surprisingly, more rewarding then the one originally envisioned. Patience, gentleness and self-control are all necessary virtues in managing change. Reflecting on the maternal practice of weaning can enable clergy to value the attention and compassion necessary to understand and address people's fears of change. It can also encourage a proper valuing of trial and error that is not afraid of failure. Managing change in this way calls for creativity and contextual knowledge; the focus is on a process that maintains the inter-subjectivity of relationships and the flourishing of the community.

Conclusion: Being and Doing

The examples in this chapter do not offer a definitive description of parish ministry, but they do point to aspects of the practice that have been under-articulated and therefore undervalued. This is particularly important in the current climate, both in and beyond the Church, where the setting and measuring of targets appears to value certain skill-sets above others. Fears about Church decline feed into the sense that clergy need to show that they are being productive while often knowing that the role has little to do with recognisable models of productivity. The dissonance between the rewarding aspects of building up communities and sustaining the ongoing round of services and parish life and the demand to define what they are doing in measurable targets can make it hard for clergy to recognise and affirm their own good practice.

This difficulty is exacerbated because clergy, like mothers, find that many of these skills are assumed to be about personality or instinctual knowledge. Thus the ability to cherish people may be dismissed with the suggestion that someone is just a good 'people person'. It is true that some people will, through personality and upbringing, find it easier to cherish people, but that is not to say it has not been learned and practised. Those for whom it does not come easily can also learn if they are prepared to practise and reflect on the practice. Cherishing is an art, a skill and a discipline. It is a practical skill, so it cannot be learned in abstract or measured through quantifiable outcomes. However, it can be experienced by those being cherished and witnessed to by their resulting flourishing. The same is true for comforting and many of the other skills I have sought to articulate above.

When clergy are not taught to value and understand these skills, they can often unintentionally damage the communities that they are entrusted to care for. They can also, through their lack of care for people, for buildings, and the processes of change, unwittingly negate the message of God's loving care that they are seeking to proclaim. For clergy, like mothers, are caught up in an immensely complex mixture of being and doing. The role is both a relationship and an activity. The relationship shapes the activity and the ongoing action shapes and develops the relationship. As a mother I do things for my children, and the kinds of things I do are shaped by the contingent reality of the children and the concrete situations of daily life. Through relying on my good enough response to their needs they are strengthened in both their sense of what a mother is and what they can expect a mother to do. The love that we share is both the motivation for the activity and a product of that ongoing reliable responsiveness. It is also, from my perspective, shaped by the sheer wonder of seeing my labour and action sustaining the unique lives that are growing into maturity.

In parish ministry the priest is in a relationship to the parish and that relationship shapes the actions and the actions shape the relationship. The kinds of skills described in this chapter sustain and encourage the flourishing of life. Cherishing, comforting, multi-attending and storytelling all develop and deepen the relationship as the priest seeks to know and care for these people in the concrete and contingent circumstances of their lives. Through good housekeeping skills she maintains the space they need to develop and mature in faith. Some will need a lot of practical help; others are at a stage when, so long as the resources are made available, they can cater for themselves, and possibly for others, including the priest.

Through attending well to the concrete and the particular, clergy can learn to understand the complex feelings that connect to buildings, objects, styles of worship and faith practices. They can then realise that in change the *process* is vitally important. They can learn the art of weaning: helping people to manage change in ways that enable them to feel secure. They can translate feelings into words or rituals, recognising that many aspects of people's beliefs are held through embodied practices and non-verbal ways of knowing. And because it is about a relationship, they can reflect on how their own habits and practices shape their responses and actions. Through such practice a clergy character is developed. This cannot simply be understood as an internal process of being. It is lived out in an endless round of doing. From the smallest tasks to the large and momentous decisions, we shape the relationships we have with others. How we act is shaped by the way we think and what we value. How the relationships we have flourish depends on how we act in them.

There are many different tasks that make up the work of a parish priest and this means that clergy have a lot to do. They therefore need to be good managers, good administrators and, at times, a good general dogsbody. What matters is the motivational starting point. It is through attending lovingly to the people entrusted to a priest's care that these tasks are acted on. To lose sight of the reality of the inter-subjective relationship means that organising, managing and leading can all too easily degenerate into a relationship of subject/object in which the people are seen simply as the led. One of the temptations of ministry is to gravitate towards tasks that seem to provide measurable and tangible outcomes, thus projects, be they buildings or other kinds of initiatives, can feel satisfying, as they hold the prospect of an assessable end. Yet the primary task is to build up the people of God, and this is ongoing. It can be assessed to some extent by looking at the flourishing of the people. Are they healthy? Yet how this question is asked and assessed is also important because it must not lose sight of the particularity of these people in this place and the centrality of the relationship between clergy and people.

For parish clergy, understanding the temptation to look for more easily definable goals is important. So, too, is resisting the alternative temptation of assuming somehow that any planning or strategies are unnecessary for God will somehow do it all. Finding ways to look for the signs of God's kingdom in the people and places where they minister involves accepting glimpses and surprises rather than finished products. As Ruddick says of maternal practice, to name virtues and ways of thinking is not to necessarily possess them; it is about highlighting the struggles and naming the temptations. Both children and congregations are resilient. While serious neglect, bullying or abuse can all cause lasting damage and should be named as wrong, the more straightforward failures of mothering and ministry are survivable. In fact, the ability to learn from our inadequacies and mistakes is one of the values that we need to pass on to those in our care. As Arendt reminds us, the ability to forgive and to be forgiven is an essential aspect of human action and interaction. As is the willingness to make promises and start anew.

In writing about parish ministry I may well be accused of neglecting important aspects of the role, such as teaching and preaching, leading worship and administering the Sacraments and engaging in mission. I do not want to suggest that these are not important. The formal ways in which the faith is taught and reflected on are necessary aspects of building up the Church and individual Christians. Parish clergy need to find authentic ways to handle scripture and tradition, to engage with the ongoing story of God's involvement with his people and to help people themselves grow in the virtues of Christian discipleship. However, I would maintain that clergy can be tempted to overestimate the value of their didactic teaching and to undervalue the ways people learn through the wider aspects of parish life and ministry. A failure to acknowledge this means that clergy can feel frustrated if they concentrate on the formal, didactic ways of imparting the faith while neglecting all the unconscious or unarticulated learning that is happening around them. Theologically literate and powerfully delivered sermons about the generous welcome of God will be diminished by an inhospitable vicarage and a permanently locked church.

Plenty of parish priests, like plenty of mothers, are 'good enough'. They may not be consciously thinking about their practice in the kinds of ways that have been articulated. However, a genuine love of the people they care for has enabled them to develop a practical wisdom that means that often enough they respond appropriately to meet the contingent needs of the other with an attitude that enables them to flourish. They will draw on human skills of comforting and caring, finding out over time what works well and how to be comfortable with different people in difficult circumstances. They will reflect on the feelings of others and on their own feelings and use them to make judgements about appropriate behaviour. Yet if they are not encouraged to value such thinking, reflecting and learning, they may fail to see that these are some of the best aspects of their ministry. Stadlen says this about mothering:

> There are many books prescribing what a mother should achieve ... But there isn't much that explores what mothers do achieve. If there were, we should have more words or phrases to describe motherly achievements. The result is that many mothers do not recognise their own successes.[14]

My concern is that we fail to articulate the achievements of good parish ministry, which involves all the seemingly unproductive aspects of being seen around the parish, being interruptible, knowing how to offer a comforting word or attend properly to friend and stranger. The process of keeping the show going, noticing if the church is clean and the aspect welcoming, putting on the services with love and attention, being authentic, trustworthy, humble, cheerful and faithful. If we undervalue all these things and appear to privilege formulaic action plans and blueprints for growth then I would suggest we undermine the proper practice of parish ministry and its vital importance for building up the church in a particular place. We also make it hard for clergy to recognise their own successes and take pleasure and joy in all that they do.

---

[14]   Stadlen, *What Mothers Do*, p. 13.

Conclusion

In this book I have looked at how mothering can be understood and how priesthood can be better articulated by utilising a maternal metaphor. Both practices consist of a relationship and an activity. There are of course ways in which mothering and ministry are very different. Clergy are in many cases paid and have to deal with complex issues around fundraising and balancing the books out of congregational giving. They also move, thus they are often in a fostering role nurturing a community for a time and then having to negotiate leaving and handing on. Yet, it is my contention that the maternal metaphor offers a rich way of articulating the relationship and activity that is at the heart of parochial ministry, offering insights into how clergy can think about what they do. The metaphor also helps to identify the difficulty clergy have in talking meaningfully about many aspects of ministry and thus why good practice often goes un-affirmed and under-valued.

The Problem of Essentialism and Complementarity

Aspects of mothering and ministry have unintentionally been silenced by the language of essentialism and ontology. Such an understanding can unwittingly imply that the work of each should flow naturally out of their being. For mothers this is described as a maternal instinct and for priests the grace or character of ordination. I would suggest that in both cases this language fails to acknowledge the actual process of learning how to practise the role, leading to under-articulation of the skills practitioners develop. It can also lead to high levels of guilt when what should flow naturally is difficult to learn; mothers and priests can perceive themselves to be failing where love and service is a struggle.

However, when essentialist ideas are totally dismissed in favour of equality in terms of gender or all member ministry, there tends to be an unintentional silencing of the reality of difference, which is problematic. In gender theories, I argue, it silences the specific experience of mothering with its connection to women's bodies and the reality that childcare has been seen as women's work. This has also led to a lack of recognition of the skills developed and the rewards present in caring for children. In theologies of ministry, to silence the difference of ordination, by rightfully affirming the ministry of all, leads to a genuine confusion about the role of the priest and an uncertainty about the kind of language and models appropriate for the role. This may lead to avoiding specifically priestly language and speaking more generally about leadership, and possibly borrowing models from secular organisations. However, the motivation to affirm the ministry of all does not seem to have produced a better way of speaking about the laity or of collaborative patterns of ministry.

Ministry and mothering are relational and must be understood as such. Being and doing, ontology and activity need to be held together through a proper understanding of inter-subjective relationships. Looking at the mother–child relationship can, I suggest, provide a way of understanding difference through a caring relationship that although asymmetric involves two subjects. From the earliest point in the relationship mother and child look for mutual recognition and begin to develop a way of adapting and negotiating with each other. Although the child is dependent on the mother this does not negate the inter-subjectivity. The child plays her part in shaping the relationship through her responses to the mother's care. A second child may provide a similar relationship, but any mother would tell you that this new baby is a different person and therefore new ways of negotiating and adapting to this child must be learnt. The relationship is particular; the mother and child are real people, not generic models. It also requires constant adaptation as the child grows and develops. A mother may mourn the passing of various stages but she understands and fosters her child's growth and development. It is a relationship of care that involves contingent response-ability. Dependence, in such a caring relationship, is real, but it is always transitional. The relationship moves into complex patterns of dependence and interdependence as the child grows and develops.

By using a maternal imagery to look at parish ministry I have suggested that it is principally a relationship of caring responsibility. The priest has this relationship with a particular community or communities in and through which people can grow and mature in their Christian faith. Within these communities there will be relationships of mutuality, but there will also be asymmetrical relationships in which the priest provides the luxury of transitional dependence. In such encounters she is there for the other providing the care they need at this time and she finds reciprocity through seeing the other accept and benefit from her care. Doing so she understands that God's grace flows through such human acts of compassionate kindness and finds her ministry validated by the ways in which individuals grow in their understanding of God's love and care. The multiplicity of such relationships means that a priest has to develop the capacity to read people and situations quickly so that she can respond appropriately, comforting, cherishing, challenging and sustaining the people she encounters. This requires the ability to attend properly to people, to compassionately feel with them while not losing herself in the feelings, instead offering a perspective and a caring presence. This reading of people and feeling with and for them requires a kind of reasoning that takes feelings seriously. Feelings become a necessary part of reasoning, enabling responsive action and assessing of that action. Thinking and feeling are not in opposition, but partnership.

In caring for others, both mothers and priests provide the places necessary for people to find the security to refresh themselves and establish who they are. Within homes and churches people are fed and taught. They find the familiar spaces and objects, the family stories and rituals that help them to make sense of themselves in the world. A parish priest needs to take seriously the homemaking aspect of maintaining a church and its services, ensuring that, as far as possible, the faithful are sustained and encouraged to grow, while visitors and newcomers are made welcome. I have suggested that attention needs to be paid to the non-verbal language of the buildings, services and people in the church. It is important to understand how much people learn through these non-verbal messages and to ensure, as far as possible, that they do not undermine the formal teaching and mission of the church.

To see parish ministry through a maternal metaphor has allowed me to suggest that Ruddick's language of a threefold demand and consequent temptations and virtues can offer a constructive reflection on the actual experience of parish ministry. Parish priests have the responsibility for preserving the life and faith of those entrusted to their care, fostering growth in individuals and the community and educating in the Christian faith. The latter correlates to Ruddick's concept of acceptability, in this case to the wider Church and, primarily, aiming for all to be acceptable to God. In response to these demands clergy need to develop ways of thinking and virtues that enable them to act well contingently, responding appropriately to the real people and places in their care. Both mothering and ministry are teleological, they are aiming for maturity both in their own practice and in the people they are caring for. Mothers want to be 'good enough' and they want their children to grow up into reasonable people. Clergy are called to play their part in being good enough as they build up the Church, the body of Christ.

The virtue of humility is central to both practices. Clergy need to practise humility to guard against the temptations of domination or abnegation of responsibility; the temptation to over-intrusive ministry or of neglect. Both of these may be motivated by good intentions but they are failures in inter-subjectivity. The priest may seek to impose her will on others for their own good, or to be constantly trying to involve herself in lives at an intrusive level in order to meet her own sense of being needed. She may also fail to make decisions or act in ways consonant with her responsibilities because she is wary of responsibility or because she allows others to dominate. Parish priests need to be hopeful, compassionate and trustworthy, as they guard against the temptations to an unrealistic cheeriness, inauthenticity or despair and passivity.

In taking their responsibility seriously they must learn to delight in the achievements of others and learn to cherish even those they find it hard to like. Such behaviour is both virtue and discipline. In doing this they draw on their theological understanding of the worth of each person in God's sight and the sense of people as gifts, however strange. Above all, they need to develop the virtue of *phronesis*, the intellectual virtue of acting well in contingent circumstances. This virtue is developed through the practice and the ability to reflect on experience and grow in wisdom. Reflection benefits from the input of others; through conversations and storytelling wisdom is built up. This includes the willingness to share failures as an aspect of learning and, as Arendt points out, requires the capacity to forgive and be forgiven.

Arendt's definitions of labouring, work and action offer insights into the working life of a parish priest. There is plenty of labouring; work that is necessary for sustaining life. It is cyclical and can feel mundane and menial, the job is never done. This labouring can and should be shared, but it must be valued. Noting who is doing it, thanking them and affirming its value is fundamental. This is the realm of servants, and a priest needs to understand how much of ministry involves this ongoing service and what their part is in it. Alongside and interwoven with this labouring is what Arendt describes as action, the building up of community, the speaking and acting between people. This involves collaboration: working with others and respecting their otherness, using power to generate new life and resisting the familiar temptation to dominate or allow others to dominate. The virtues of faith hope and love play their part in good collaboration, as respect for the reality of the other is maintained even where it leads to disagreement and conflict. Compassion is necessary for understanding why people feel strongly about certain issues and the skills of weaning may be necessary for managing change in ways that all can own. Action is always open-ended and allows for the surprise of new beginnings and new possibilities.

Arendt's definition of work is the aspect of human activity that should have least priority in parish ministry. There will, of course, be projects that are begun and ended with tangible results, but the ongoing work of parish life has no end and its success is to be seen in the flourishing of lives, an inexact science that requires a priest to develop an ability to attend well to people and feelings. This does not mean that strategies, visions and plans are not part of ministry, but it does mean that they have to be collaboratively developed, adaptive and open-ended. They arise out of the ongoing life of the parish and its concern to be the Church in that place.

In a culture that values the 'fabrication' model of work in which measurable targets and action plans have become part of many organisations, from manufacturing to healthcare and education, it can be difficult for clergy to live with the very different pattern of work required from ministerial practice. The boundaries are blurred and the reality of people can make it hard to evaluate success and even to define what is 'work' and what is not. This means re-evaluating the worth of time spent chatting, pondering and wandering round the parish, which can look like doing nothing to others and even, at times, to the priest herself. There are also the aspects of praying for people, which the priest knows is valuable but is, again, hard to measure in terms of efficacy or, at times, to explain to those beyond the Church. A priest needs to make time to attend to God, just as she needs to make time to attend to people. Both are in some sense intangible, sometimes the rewards of either attention are recognisable and affirmative, but a priest also needs to accept that there is much of what she does that will bear fruit slowly and she may never see or know the outcomes this side of Heaven. The rewards of ministry can be surprising and may be missed if the priest is not attending to what is around her. Above all she asks herself the question: Is it well with the people entrusted to my care? There is always more that could be done, but am I doing a good enough job to keep them safe, help them grow and fit them for the kingdom of Heaven?

Living with Ambiguity

When parish ministry goes well it is deeply rewarding but it can also be hard work and at times seem unrewarding and unappreciated. Thus clergy have to make sense of feeling at times frustrated and fed up with a role which they believe God has called them to do. The process of discernment and selection before training involves examining this sense of calling. To believe that one is called by God to be ordained and to have that belief confirmed by the processes of the particular denomination means that to be a priest carries an element of obedience. It is also seen to be a special calling and a privilege. Individuals have often given up other professions or possibilities to dedicate themselves to the life of a priest. Yet the reality of the working life of a parish priest is that it does not always feel special and clergy can have ambivalent feelings about the people and places they care for, the wider Church and even, at times, the God who has called them. Such ambivalent feelings may not be fully recognised or articulated. Feelings of frustration, boredom, anger and disappointment towards people one is supposed to love and cherish can be hard to admit. For clergy who feel called and specially blessed by God for the task of ministry, such feelings may seem to be inappropriate to their calling and signs of their sinfulness or inadequacy.

The way that mothers and ministers arrive in their roles is very different yet they are both dealing with expectations of the fulfilment to be gained from the role and the belief that love and commitment will somehow flow from them. In recent years much has been written about ambivalence in mothers and how the reality of the experience is for many so different from what they had expected. Such writing is a corrective to idealised images of motherhood that assume maternal love and care comes naturally to all mothers and that all women should feel fulfilled by their mothering role. The contrast between a general language about self-fulfilment and the ideals of mother love can present new mothers with a difficult adjustment. There are parallels between this maternal ambivalence and the experience of clergy faced with the realities of day to day ministry.

The reality for most clergy is that aspects of ministry will be rewarding, and that individual people and particular encounters will offer palpable experiences of God's grace flowing. Joy can be found in the ways that people and places grow and flourish, in simple things done well and in generous efforts appreciated. Clergy will come to love and be loved by individuals and communities. Yet at the same time there will be frustrations, difficult people and lack of appreciation, feelings of marginalisation, rejection and manipulation. As I have argued above, some of this can be as a result of the priest's own inability to respect and work collaboratively with others, setting up struggles of domination and submission. But much will simply be the result of working in a role where there is always more to be done and measures of success are often intangible.

What de Marneffe says of mothering may well ring true for many clergy as they reflect on parish ministry:

> It is hard sometimes to feel recognised for the value of our work in the day-to-day activity of mothering. And anything that makes our sense of competence more tenuous can evoke doubts about our effectiveness and worth in an even stronger way.[1]

She makes the valuable point that often tiredness, a multiplicity of things to be done and the social sense that others do not see and recognise the efforts one is making, can all add to doubts about the efficacy of the practice. Yet, the reality is that when the practice does not involve the tangible end products of Arendt's work, but instead involves the ongoing labour of sustaining life and the complex action of building relationships, it is always going to be harder to assess success. And when the fruits of one's efforts may take a long time to emerge, it can be hard to know whether time and energy spent has been well used. De Marneffe goes on to say:

> If our self-esteem comes from doing our job well, then the taxing demands and divided attention motherhood introduces can make us feel like we do everything badly.[2]

Again these words about mothering ring true for parish ministry, where the pressures of pastoral needs are not controllable and the build-up of responsibilities at some times can lead to exhaustion and a feeling that nothing is being done to the standard one expects of oneself, let alone what we believe God expects of us. It is at these times in ministry when people can become irritants, or worse, and the temptation to dominating patterns of control can feel like a useful way of preserving time and energy.

For clergy, the added dimension of obedience to God means that ambivalent feelings and concerns about efficacy in ministry can lead to doubts about their calling or their openness to God. The language used about ministry plays a significant part in the expectations of others and of the priest herself. If she is to be a servant to God and to others, how does she address feelings of being undervalued and under-appreciated? If self-sacrifice is central to Christian theology, how can she complain about being overworked? If she is to love and care for those whom God loves, what does she do about the people she dislikes? If she is to pronounce God's forgiveness, how does she deal with those who have hurt her and let her down? And since everything is caught up in the ongoing work of God's grace, how does she begin to know what is happening because of her and what would simply happen despite her? All of these myriad questions can, on a bad day, leave clergy feeling uncertain about themselves and the adequacy of their ministry.

I have argued that a sense of self-respect and subjectivity is important for a priest in order for her to be able to minister well. Isolation and a lack of opportunity

---

[1]   de Marneffe, *Maternal Desire*, p. 120.

[2]   Ibid.

to talk honestly and meaningfully to other practitioners can erode self-confidence and skew perceptions. Clergy need people who can help them get their perspective on the parish and its myriad problems. They need people who can help them refocus on God, as one who loves and values them, not as one who expects more than they can give. These people come in various forms: family and friends – inside and beyond the parish, colleagues – inside or beyond the parish, spiritual directors and theological mentors. Ruddick notes that mothers can misidentify virtues and can mischaracterise success and failure because of their own and others' expectations of the role.[3] This same misidentifying is an ever-present reality of parish ministry.

Thus clergy need the kinds of relationships with others that help to correct such misidentification and to recognise their own and others' good practice. It is in this area that, I would suggest, the hierarchy of the Church needs to find better ways of caring for the clergy. Unfortunately, in many instances, it is lack of recognition from the senior clergy that can exacerbate the sense of being under-appreciated. Diocesan initiatives can appear to simply add pressures to the clergy, often unintentionally implying that there are better ways to do parish ministry with little consideration of context and particularity. The recent introduction of appraisals in most dioceses, and ministerial development reviews as part of the new terms and conditions of the Church of England, are intended to address some of these issues. However, in reality there is a lot of poor practice, and the hierarchical nature of such reviews in many dioceses can militate against an honest discussion of the difficult feelings around ministry. I would also suggest that, as in mothering, a failure to find the kind of language that can affirm the everyday, ongoing work of building and maintaining relationships and communities can mean that appraisals focus on the wrong kind of questions and can sometimes add to an individual's feeling of inadequacy.[4]

The reality is that clergy are ordinary human beings working with people who bring their own characters and insecurities into the complex community of church and parish. The ongoing pressures of working in a job that is never done will inevitably mean that there are times when it feels overwhelming and perhaps impossible. Inherited patterns of ministry that favour isolation can place unreasonable expectations on individuals to do and be everything. Such unrealistic expectations and lack of sharing will inevitably compound the pressures and potential sense of inadequacy. The conflation of theological ideas of sacrifice with an unfocused, continuing sense of self-denial can make it hard for clergy to even seek and accept the affirmation that they need to keep going. 'Cheery denial' from others about the genuine costs of ministry will undermine the reality of generous self-giving. The palpable rewards of ministry can be manifold, but are not arrived at without commitment and hard work, which needs to be better named

---

[3] Ruddick, *Maternal Thinking*, p. 104.

[4] See my chapter, 'What Clergy Do: Especially When it Looks like Nothing', in Martyn Percy and Christina Rees, (eds), *Apostolic Women, Apostolic Authority* (Norwich 2010), pp. 137–46.

and honoured. Clergy also live with the double demand to respond appropriately to the expectations of those they minister to and to live up to the trust that God has placed in them.

As with mothering, there are no blueprints for how to be a good priest or build a healthy church. There are examples of good practice, the wisdom of the tradition, the insights of other practitioners, the things learned through trial and error. There are books that can help and courses that can offer new ways of looking at things and challenge one's own misconceptions. There are plenty of good ideas, helpful suggestions for managing the labouring aspects of the work, for thinking about how to enable better collaboration, better teaching, better use of the space or the liturgy of the Church. Yet all of this has to be lived out in concrete reality. A priest and those she collaborates with in caring for *this* church and *this* people in *this* context, needs to discern what the appropriate action is here and now. She needs to know the people and place and listen hard to those who may know them and understand them better; she needs to understand what she is called on to teach in terms of the apostolic faith and how best to convey those truths to these people. She needs to understand that her life is a public witness to the reality of God's grace and the possibility of becoming more Christ-like, so she must try to be authentic, trustworthy and have integrity, yet knowing that she will not always get it right and that it is enough to be 'good enough'. Her mistakes and failings can become part of a wisdom learned through trial and error as she grows through the forgiveness of God and those she serves. Above all, she needs to find a way of loving and cherishing these people and this community because God loves them and God has called her to care for them. This does not mean turning a blind eye to faults and failings; it is not an unrealistic fantasy, but a realistic acceptance of who they are and what they need in terms of preservation, fostering growth and training in the Christian faith.

It is my intention in this book to affirm many aspects of good practice in parish ministry and to acknowledge that many priests attend well to the reality of their parishes and respond appropriately often enough to be trusted. They may not name the virtues or temptations, but their care and concern for the people and communities entrusted to them means that they are developing virtues like humility and compassion while recognising the need to resist imposing their will or failing to take responsibility appropriately. These priests may not use the terminology of comforting and cherishing people, but they simply see it as part of the job. For some the practice of ministry has meant they have become virtuous and to act well contingently feels natural. Such priests can be male or female and will have learned to care from a variety of different backgrounds. I have been privileged to know and work with such caring priests and see the flourishing that such care engenders.

However, the very ease with which some priests are able to care and comfort, to provide a homely church and encourage maturity in those they encounter can hide the hard learning and honing of skills involved. It can sometimes mistakenly be assumed that it is all about a given personality. It is my contention that good practices can be learnt and developed. Past personal experience and natural disposition can make aspects of ministry easier for some than others, but virtues can be practised by all. Attending properly to others, respecting them and caring for them involves human capacities and skills that can be honed and improved.

In highlighting these aspects of ministry that have been under-articulated and thus overlooked, I am suggesting that they have a centrality to both sustaining the faithful and reaching out in mission. Acknowledging that human beings learn as much, if not more, from the non-didactic and non-verbal, I am encouraging clergy to attend more closely to the *habitus* they help create and to the signals they send out through their own lives and bodies. I do not want to undermine the value of good preaching and teaching. The didactic teaching needs to be of the best quality possible for people to be able to engage with the ongoing story of God's loving involvement with the world and to make connections between their own lives and the calling to be virtuously Christian. Ensuring that the regular worship is of a high standard is also vital for all of the community to experience their dependence on God and to receive the spiritual feeding necessary for growth. Where the regular worship is good many will take up little of the priest's time, being able to experience God and draw the nourishment they need from word and sacrament. But all of this involves recognising and valuing the wealth of unspoken messages that the building, people and priest send out both to the faithful and to the visitors.

The purpose of this book has been to offer a maternal model for the role of a parish priest. I am not suggesting that this is the only model, but I am suggesting that it can offer insights into the role, particularly seeing the role as a relationship and activity that is about contingent, responsive care. If a priest cares for his or her parish as a mother tenderly, what does this mean? I have suggested that it means she practises attentive care, seeking to know when to respond and how to respond appropriately within the contingencies present in real communities and encounters with real people. She does this believing that the grace of God, revealed in Jesus Christ, flows through genuine acts of compassion and that she has been called to witness to the reality of this grace. She leads where appropriate because she cares. She teaches and nurtures because she cares. She manages the organisational aspects necessary to ensure that the church provides a place where people can rest on God, be spiritually fed and emotionally cherished. She practises hospitality and comforts those in need. She delights in all the different achievements of the others in the community, even when they may be far from the things that would normally be of interest to her. She forgives and is forgiven for failures in attention that lead to inappropriate response or neglect. And she conveys hope in word and deed. Hope in the reality of God's love, hope in the possibilities of redeemed humanity, hope in the reality of forgiveness and new birth, and hope in the eschatological promises that, in the end, we will know and experience what it is to be fully grown up in Christ.

Such virtuous practice cannot be learned in abstract. Preparation and good teaching can help, but most important is the experience of practice and the ability to reflect on and learn from such experience. It therefore follows that the training period for clergy post-ordination is particularly important. The role of a training incumbent in helping such reflection and modelling good practice should provide a supportive learning environment. As should the whole congregation in a training parish, giving constructive feedback, affirming what is good and gently naming and forgiving what is lacking or inappropriate. Unfortunately, beyond the curacy clergy are still often isolated in their role, and provision for self-assessment and continued learning are limited and formalised. Finding ways of enabling opportunities for clergy to meet together and chat un-defensively is important. They need spaces and places to share the stories of success and failure and to learn from the reaction of others to their stories and from the stories of others. Finding language that affirms the aspects of ministry I have been stressing, that is about caring for people rather than creating projects, is necessary if clergy are going to value for themselves the kinds of things that make their ministry flourish.

It follows that clergy need to *feel* cherished by the diocesan hierarchy and systems rather than pressured into producing formulaic responses. They need to be recognised as individuals working in individual places. If they feel under-valued and unrecognised they are more likely to be tempted to find a sense of worth through asserting their status over the laity or feeding their need to be needed by intrusive ministry, creating cultures of dependency. Where the parish priest has a sense of her subjectivity and a recognition of the subjectivity of those she cares for, she will find a rich mix of relationships. These will include relationships that demand care, provide care for her, delight and surprise, frustrate and hurt, forgive and start again, as she and they learn to resist the temptations and grow in virtue, allowing the grace of God to flow in them and between them, blessing and sanctifying. And both she, in her public witness as a priest, and others, in their witness as Christians, will make manifest the glory of God at work in the world.

Bibliography

Advisory Council for the Church's Mission (ACCM) (1987), 'Education for the Church's Ministry', occasional paper No. 22, London: Church House.

ACCM (1990), 'Ordination and the Church's Ministry: A Theological Evaluation', republished as Advisory Board for Ministry (ABM) (1991), paper No. 1, London: Church House.

Arendt, H. (1958; 2nd edn 1998), *The Human Condition*, Chicago, IL: University of Chicago Press.

Beattie, T. (2006), *New Catholic Feminism*, Abingdon: Routledge.

Belenky, M.F., Clinchy, B.M., Goldberger, N.R. and Tarule, J.M. (1986), *Women's Ways of Knowing*, New York, NY: Basic Books.

Benjamin, J. (1988), *The Bonds of Love: Psychoanalysis, Feminism and the Problem of Domination*, New York, NY: Pantheon.

Benjamin, J. (1995), *Like Subjects, Love Objects: Essays on Recognition and Sexual Difference*, New Haven, CT: Yale University Press.

Best, E. (1972), *A Commentary on First and Second Thessalonians*, London: Black.

BMU (1986), *The Priesthood of the Ordained Ministry*.

Buber, M. (1970, 2nd edn), *I and Thou*, Edinburgh: T&T Clark.

Butler, Judith (1990), *Gender Trouble: Feminism and the Subversion of Identity*, London: Routledge.

Call to Order (1989), ACCM.

Calvin, John (2002 electronic edn), *John Calvin Works and Correspondence*, Charlottesville, VA: Intelex Corporation.

Carr, A.E. (1988), *Transforming Grace*, London: Harper Row.

Carr, W. (1985), *The Priestlike Task*, London: SPCK.

Chodorow, N. (1978; new edn 1999), *The Reproduction of Mothering*, Berkeley, CA: University of California Press.

Cocksworth, C. and Brown, R. (2002), *Being a Priest Today*, Norwich: Canterbury Press.

Common Worship, www.churchofengland.org.

Countryman, W.L. (1999), *Living on the Border*, Harrisburg, PA: Morehouse Publishing.

Croft, S. (1999; 2nd edn 2008), *Ministry in Three Dimensions*, London: Darton, Longman and Todd.

Dallavalle, N.A. (1998), 'Toward a Theology that is Catholic and Feminist', *Modern Theology*, vol. 14, No. 4 (October), pp. 535–53.

Daly, M. (1990), 'The Looking-Glass Society', in A. Loades (ed.), *Feminist Theology: A Reader*, Louisville, KY: Westminster/John Knox Press, pp. 189–92.

Davison, A. and Milbank, A. (2010), *For the Parish: A Critique of Fresh Expressions*, London: SCM.

Farmer, J. (2005), 'Ministry and Worship', in D. Marmion and M. Hines (eds), *The Cambridge Companion to Rahner*, Cambridge: Cambridge University Press, pp. 144–57.

Farrer, A. (2006), 'Walking Sacraments', in A. Loades, and R. MacSwain (eds), *The Truth Seeking Heart*, Norwich: Canterbury Press, pp. 138–41.

Fiorenza, E.S. and Carr, A. (eds) (1989), *Motherhood: Experience, Institution, Theology* (Concilium), Edinburgh: T&T Clark.

For Such a Time as This: A Report to the General Synod of the Church of England of a Working Party of the House of Bishops (2001), London: Church House Publishing.

Galot, J. (1985), *Theology of the Priesthood*, San Francisco, CA: Ignatius Press.

Gaventa, B.R. (2007), *Our Mother St Paul*, Louisville, KY: Westminster /John Knox Press.

Gerhardt, S. (2004), *Why Love Matters: How Affection Shapes a Baby's Brain*, Hove: Brunner-Routledge.

Gill-Austern, B. (1996), 'Love Understood as Self-Sacrifice and Self-Denial: What Does it Do to Women?', in J. Stevenson Moessner (ed.), *Through the Eyes of Women*, Minneapolis, MN: Augsburg Fortress Press, pp. 304–21.

Gilligan, C. (1982), *In a Different Voice: Psychological Theory and Women's Development*, Cambridge, MA: Harvard University Press.

Green, A. (2009), *A Theology of Women's Priesthood*, London: SPCK.

Greenwood, R. (1994), *Transforming Priesthood*, London: SPCK.

Gregory I, Pope (1908), *S. Gregory on the Pastoral Charge: The Benedictine Text*, translated by Henry Ramsden Bramley, Oxford: J. Parker.

Grenholm, C. (2011), *Motherhood and Love*, Cambridge: Eerdmans.

Gudorf, C. (1985), 'Parenting, Mutual Love and Sacrifice', in B.H. Andolsen et al. (eds), *Women's Consciousness, Women's Conscience*, Minneapolis, MN: Seabury Books/Winston Press, pp. 175–91.

Guiver, G. (ed.) (2001), *Priests in a People's Church*, London: SPCK.

Gunton, C.E.H. and Daniel, W. (eds) (1989), *On Being the Church*, Edinburgh: T&T Clark.

Hahn, C.A. (1994), *Growing in Authority: Relinquishing Control*, New York, NY: The Alban Institute.

Hanson, A. (1961), *The Pioneer Ministry*, London: SCM.

Hanson, A. (1975), *Church Sacrament and Ministry*, Oxford: Mowbrays.

Harrison, B.W. (1985), 'The Power of Anger in the Work of Love: Christian Ethics for Women and Other Strangers', in C.S. Robb (ed.), *Making the Connections*, Boston, MA: Beacon Press, pp. 3–21.

Healy, N.M. (2000), *Church, World and the Christian Life: Practical–Prophetic Ecclesiology*, Cambridge: Cambridge University Press.

Hebblethwaite, M. (1984), *Motherhood and God*, London: Geoffrey Chapman.

Holmes, U.T. (1982), *Spirituality for Ministry*, San Francisco, CA: Harper & Row.

Hrdy, S.B. (1999), *Mother Nature*, New York, NY: Pantheon.

Irigaray L. (1977), *Ce sexe qui n'en est pas un*, Paris: Minuit.

Irigaray, L. (1985), *This Sex Which Is Not One* translated by Catherine Porter, Ithaca: Cornell University Press.

Irigaray, L. (1993), *Je, Tu, Nous: Toward a Culture of Difference*, London: Routledge

Irigaray, L. (1993), *Sexes and Genealogies*, New York, NY: Columbia University Press.

John Paul II, Pope (1976), *Inter Insigniores*, 15 October, Sacred Congregation for the Doctrine of Faith, www.papalencyclicals.net.

John Paul II, Pope (1995), *Letter to Women*, 29 June, www.vatican.com.

Johnson, Elizabeth (1999). *She Who Is: The Mystery of God in Feminist Theological Discourse* (New York: Crossroad).

Jones, S. (2000), *Feminist Theory and Christian Theology: Cartographies of Grace*, Minneapolis, MN: Fortress Press.

Kilby, K. (1997), *Karl Rahner*, London: Fount.

Kilby, K. (2000) 'Perichoresis and Projection: Problems with Social Doctrines of the Trinity', *New Blackfriars*, vol. 81 (October), pp. 432–45.

de Lubac, H. (1982), *The Motherhood of the Church*, San Francisco, CA: Ignatius Press.

McFadyen, A. (1990), *The Call to Personhood*, Cambridge: Cambridge University Press.

McFague, S. (1983), *Metaphorical Theology: Models of God in Religious Language*, London: SCM.

MacIntyre, A. (1981; 3rd edn 2007), *After Virtue*, London: Duckworth.

MacIntyre, A. (1999), *Dependent Rational Animals: Why Human Beings Need the Virtues*, London: Duckworth.

Macquarrie, J. (1986), *Theology, Church and Ministry*, London: SCM.

de Marneffe, D. (2006), *Maternal Desire: On Children, Love and the Inner Life*, London: Virago.

Mauss, M. (1979), *The Notion of Body Techniques in Sociology and Psychology*, translated by Ben Brewster, London: Routledge & Kegan Paul.

Miller-McLemore, B.J. (1994), *Also a Mother*, Nashville, TN: Abingdon Press.

Miller-McLemore, B.J. (2003), *Let the Children Come*, San Francisco, CA: Jossey-Bass.

Miller-McLemore, B.J. (2007), *In the Midst of Chaos: Caring for Children as Spiritual Practice*, San Francisco, CA: Jossey-Bass.

Moberly, R.C. (1907; 2nd edn), *Ministerial Priesthood*, London: John Murray.

Moltmann, J. (1977), *The Church in the Power of the Spirit*, London: SCM.

Moltmann-Wendel, E. (1994), *I Am My Body*, London: SCM.

Moody, C. (1992), *Eccentric Ministry*, London: Darton, Longman and Todd.

Muddiman, J. (2001), *The Epistle to the Ephesians* (Black's NT Commentaries), London: Continuum.

Murdoch, I. (1970), *The Sovereignty of Good*, London: Routledge & Kegan Paul.

Noddings, N. (1984), *Caring: A Feminine Approach to Ethics and Moral Education*, Berkeley, CA: University of California Press.

Noddings, N. (2002), *Educating Moral People*, New York, NY: Teachers College Press.

Noddings, N. (2002), *Starting at Home*, Berkeley, CA: University of California Press.

Paul VI, Pope (1964), *Lumen Gentium*, Dogmatic Constitution on the Church, 21 November, www.vatican.com.

Pelikan, J. and Lehmann, H.T. (eds) (1955–72), *Luther's Works*, St Louis, MO and Philadelphia, PA: Concordia Publishing House and Fortress Press.

Percy, M. (2006), *Clergy: The Origin of the Species*, London: Continuum.

Percy, M. (2012), *The Ecclesial Canopy: Faith, Hope, Charity*, Farnham: Ashgate.

Percy, M. and Rees, C. (eds) (2010), *Apostolic Women, Apostolic Authority: Transfiguring Leadership in Today's Church*, Norwich: Canterbury Press.

Pickard, S. (2009), *Theological Foundations for Collaborative Ministry*, Farnham: Ashgate.

Porter, J. (1990), *The Recovery of Virtue*, Louisville, KY: Westminster/John Knox Press.

Porter, J. (1995), *Moral Action and Christian Ethics*, Cambridge: Cambridge University Press.

Power, D.S. (1998), *A Spiritual Theology of the Priesthood*, Edinburgh: T&T Clark.

Pritchard, J. (2007), *The Life and Work of a Priest*, London: SPCK.

Purvis, S.B. (1991), 'Mothers, Neighbours and Strangers', *Journal of Feminist Studies in Religion*, vol. 7 (Spring), pp. 19–34.

Rahner, K. (1983), *The Love of Jesus and the Love of Neighbour*, Slough: St Paul Publications.

Rahner, K. (1966), *Theological Investigations IV*, translated by Kevin Smyth, London: Darton, Longman and Todd.

Ramsey, M. (1972), *The Christian Priest Today*, London: SPCK.

Redfern, A. (1999), *Ministry and Priesthood*, London: Darton, Longman and Todd.

Reed, B. (1978), *The Dynamics of Worship*, London: Darton, Longman and Todd.

Rich, A. (1976), *Of Woman Born*, New York: Virago.

Ruddick, S. (1989), *Maternal Thinking*, Boston, MA: Beacon Press.

Ruether, R.R. (1983), *Sexism and God-Talk*, London: SCM.

Ruether, R.R. (1985), *Women-Church*, San Francisco, CA and London: Harper & Row.

Russell, A. (1980), *The Clerical Profession*, London: SPCK.

Sadgrove, M. (2008), *Wisdom and Ministry*, London: SPCK.

Sandham, C., 'The Biblical Pattern for Women's Ministry', www.reform.org.uk.

Schaus, M. (ed.) (2006), *Women and Gender in Medieval Europe: An Encyclopaedia*, London: Routledge.

Schillebeeckx, E. (1981), *Ministry: A Case for Change*, London: SCM.

Schillebeeckx, E. (1985), *The Church with a Human Face*, London: SCM.

Schumacher, M. (2004), *Women in Christ: Toward a New Feminism*, Grand Rapids, MI: Eerdmans.

Sian, M. (ed.) (1986), *Simone Weil: An Anthology*, London: Virago.

Slee, N. (2004), *Women's Faith Development*, Farnham: Ashgate.

Soskice, J.M. (1985), *Metaphor and Religious Language*, Oxford: Clarendon Press.

Soskice, J.M. (2007), *The Kindness of God: Metaphor, Gender, and Religious Language*, Oxford: Oxford University Press.

Stadlen, N. (2004), *What Mothers Do: Especially When it Looks like Nothing*, London: Piatkus.

Stringer, M.D. (1999), *On the Perception of Worship: The Ethnography of Worship in Four Christian Congregations in Manchester*, Birmingham: University of Birmingham Press.

Thomas, T. (2001), 'Becoming a Mother: Matrescence as Spiritual Formation', *Religious Education*, vol. 96 (Winter), pp. 88–105.

Towler, R. and Coxon, A. (1979), *The Fate of the Anglican Clergy: A Sociological Study*, London: Macmillan.

Treblicot, J. (ed.) (1984), *Mothering: Essays in Feminist Theory*, Totowa, NJ: Rowan & Allanheld.

Trible, P. (1978), *God and the Rhetoric of Sexuality*, London: SCM.

Walker Bynum, C. (1982), *Jesus as Mother*, Berkeley, CA: University of California Press.

Walker Bynum, C. (1987), *Holy Feast and Holy Fast*, Berkeley, CA: University of California Press.

Walsh, C., *Speaking in Different Tongues*, a Sheffield Hallam Working Paper on the Web, www.shu.ac.uk.

Watson, N. (2002), *Introducing Feminist Ecclesiology*, Sheffield: Sheffield Accademic Press.

Weil, S. (1977), *Waiting on God*, translated from the French by Emma Crauford, London: Fount.

Whitbeck, C. (1984), 'The Maternal Instinct', in J. Trebilcot, *Mothering*, Totowa, NJ: Rowan & Allanheld, pp. 185–91.

Whitford, M. (ed.) (1991), *The Irigaray Reader*, Oxford: Blackwell.

Winnicott, D.W. (1964), *The Child, the Family and the Outside World*, London: Pelican.

Winnicott, D.W. (1965), *The Maturational Process and the Facilitating Environment*, London: Hogarth.

Wright, N.T. (2010), *Virtue Reborn*, London: SPCK.

www.womenpriests.org.

Young, I.M. (1998), 'Pregnant Embodiment', in D. Welton (ed.), *Body and Flesh*, Oxford: Blackwell, pp. 274–85.

Young, I.M. (1998), 'Throwing Like a Girl', in D. Welton (ed.), *Body and Flesh*, Oxford: Blackwell, pp. 259–73.

Index